The PIE Method for Career Success

A Unique Way to Find Your Ideal Job

Daniel Porot

Use the three phases of the PIE Method in your search for your next job:

➤ Pleasure

➤ Information

➤ Employment

The PIE Method for Career Success

Copyright © 1996 by Daniel Porot

Published by JIST Works, Inc.
720 North Park Avenue
Indianapolis, IN 46202-3431
Phone 317-264-3720 Fax 317-264-3709 e-mail: JISTWorks@AOL.com

Cover Design: Doug Diedrich
Interior Design: Barbara Kordesh

Library of Congress Cataloging-in-Publication Data Applied For

Printed in the United States of America

99 98 97 96   1 2 3 4 5 6 7 8 9

Earlier edition copyright© 1992 by Cabinet Daniel Porot

ISBN: 1-56370-182-0

Acknowledgments

There are several people to whom I would like to wholeheartedly express my sincere appreciation. As authors often say, without them this book would not exist.

First of all, I would like to acknowledge the late John Crystal. He was the first to come up with the idea of gathering information prior to going to an interview. To do this, he applied the information gathering methods that he learned and practiced during World War II as a Counter Intelligence Agent to the job hunting process. I respected and admired him a lot. Our friendship was warm and spontaneous.

Next, I must thank my dear friend Dick Bolles, author of *What Color Is Your Parachute?* Dick has a unique brain which he uses to, among other things, make people laugh. He also possesses a unique heart which he uses to, among other things, surprise people with love. And he has a unique communication gift which he uses to, among other things, write and teach. We have been leading a two-week workshop together each summer for the past 15 years... and we are still friends!

The third person I would like to express my appreciation to is Mike Farr, president of JIST Works, Inc. He is a close friend who took the initiative to publish this book in the United States. I admire both the wonderful work he does and his rich personality. I respect his strong values, which are so deeply rooted within him.

These three people—John, Dick, and Mike—share a similar trait: they never take themselves too seriously!

I would also like to address a special mention to:

Debi Borst of JIST who dedicated long hours polishing and editing the text of this book;

Barb Kordesh who had the uneasy task of incorporating the right brain portion of this book (graphics) with the left brain portion (text);

and finally, Leo Casement, John Webb, and everyone else who contributed to this book.

Thank you all so much!

Foreword

By Richard N. Bolles, author

What Color Is Your Parachute?

> **Editor's Comment**
>
> *What Color Is Your Parachute?* is the best selling career planning and job search book ever written. Its author, Richard Bolles, is one of the founders of a movement that has come to be called "Life/Work Planning." Each year Bolles and a small group of presenters conduct a two-week workshop on Life/Work Planning for career counselors and job seekers.

For more than 20 years, I have been leading an annual two-week workshop, to which people come from all over the world. For many years I looked for someone who could share that teaching and leadership with me. My criteria was simple: he (or she) must be brilliant, a fabulous teacher, endlessly creative, a person possessed of "soul," someone who listened well, had great compassion for job hunters, was total master of his or her field, and had a tremendous sense of humor.

It took me five years to find such a person. He (for it turned out to be a "he") came to me from another country (in fact, another continent)—Europe. His name: Daniel Porot, a Frenchman teaching in Switzerland and France. For the past 16 years, Daniel has cotaught the annual workshop with me. Each year, it is great fun for me to watch as he dazzles the workshop participants with his drawing, his clever analogies, and his flashing wit. His mastery of his field is total and absolute. I know of no one in the world who is his equal. Each year he comes to the workshop fresh from having toiled all year long helping individual job hunters with the problems they present and finding new and imaginative ways to solve those job-hunting problems. I always learn from him, every time we are together.

Of course, the number of people who can attend the annual workshop here in the United States is limited to 60, so most of the country has no access to his brilliant teaching. This is a sad thing. Hence, my great joy that JIST is now publishing Daniel in the United States. This will make him accessible to many more U.S. job hunters and career counselors, and this is great news for us.

I have referred to Daniel's PIE method in *What Color Is Your Parachute?* for a number of years now, but only briefly. Here, at last, is a full explanation of what he teaches. I commend this book to you with the highest recommendation.

Table of Contents

INTRODUCTION

Selecting a Good Job — an Important Task!

Planning your career and making good job decisions are important throughout your life. Consider the kinds of decisions you will make (or have made) at various points in your working life.

■ When you are 20 years old

At this age, your career decisions will affect the next 45 years of your life.

That's 11,250 working days!

The choice you make here is often one of your first major life decisions and may be of great importance.

■ When you are 30 years old

This decision will affect 35 years of your life and 8,750 working days!

An error made here can cost you a lot of income and satisfaction!

■ When you are 40 years old

At 40, your decision will affect another 25 years of your life! That is 6,250 working days! This age is often a pivotal point in one's professional life.

■ When you are 50 years old

Any decision reached now will affect 15 years of your life, representing 3,750 working days! You don't want to make a mistake here and regret it later.

■ When you are 60 years old

At this age, your decision will affect your life for 5 or more years and at least 1,250 working days. The decisions you make here will prepare you for retirement, so they can be very important.

You will face career decisions throughout your professional life. The choices you make will help determine your earnings and your happiness. It is logical to reach such important decisions with good information and preparation. Spending time planning your career will result in better decisions now and in the future.

The Major Steps of the PIE Process

You started school when you were about 5 years old and probably finished between the ages of 18-22. This represents approximately 2,250 days (15 years at 150 days per year) of education. Those days filled your head with information, but during your entire education, how much time did you actually devote to:

- ➤ identifying which profession turns you on?

- ➤ defining your ideal job?

- ➤ planning a strategy to find this job? and,

- ➤ eventually convincing someone to hire you?

Most education spends far too little time on these important issues. If your education did not prepare you to handle them, the book in your hands will. It is organized into eight chapters.

Chapter One: The Traditional Ways to Choose a Job

This chapter presents the 16 methods used most often to choose a career direction. Includes the pros and cons of each method.

Chapter Two: The Key Criteria for Your Next Job

You will learn the key factors to consider when defining jobs, and how to narrow down job options to those that hold the strongest appeal for you. You will also be shown how to specify those jobs that suit you best.

Chapter Three: The Two Key Components of Your Job: Title and Field

You will gain a better understanding of job titles and industries and realize that the options available to you are much greater than you might think.

Chapter Four: Your Ideal Title: Crossroads of Your Talents

This chapter helps you identify your talents and skills, and discover those that are particularly important to you. These are usually the ones you excel in or that excite you when you are using them. These key skills and talents help build a basis for defining your ideal job.

Chapter Five: Your Preferred Field: Crossroads of Your Interests

Through a creative and fun process, you will identify career areas that attract you most. You will then include them in your career planning to help you make better long-term decisions.

Chapter Six: Your Target Job: Title and Field Combined

You will combine what you have learned in previous chapters to determine the specific jobs for which you are best suited. The "ideal" job, once it is defined, will form the basis for your search for it.

Chapter Seven: The PIE Method

This chapter helps you understand and use the PIE Method. It is proven to be the simplest and most effective method for:

- ➤ Determining what you really want;

- ➤ Avoiding dead-end or unsatisfying jobs; and

- ➤ Convincing an employer to hire you.

Chapter Eight: Some Golden Rules and Advice to Ensure Your Success

Prevention is always better than a cure, and this chapter provides tips on succeeding in a new job, and how to move up to higher levels of responsibility and skill as you progress.

1

THE TRADITIONAL WAYS TO CHOOSE A JOB

Some jobs you dream about, others you envy, certain ones pay well, and still others offer respectability or prestige. What factors will affect your career decision?

The Traditional Ways to Choose a Job

How much does data processing pay?

I know one thing — I don't (or do) want to be like my mom and dad!

This degree is my ticket to a good job!

These short and simple statements summarize the way many people make career decisions. But, the job in which you are going to spend:

1/3 of your time and

1/3 of your life

deserves to be chosen with a little more reflection.

Too often, people are careless or lazy when making career decisions. Without giving it much thought, they make decisions that can last a lifetime.

Although this may be the traditional way people make these decisions, this is really not career design at all.

The following pages present various methods which are traditionally used to make career plans. You will recognize some of them as those used by a friend, relative, parent, or maybe even yourself. Each method has its own advantages and disadvantages. Later, you will see another way… a better way.

■ This is what my parents did

Your grandfather or grandmother was a...

your father or mother is a...

therefore, you will be a...

Parents (or you) often assume that you should follow a career path similar to their own. It can seem to be as strong a given as your genetic makeup.

PROS

- This is a very easy choice to make.
- You will often have the approval and support of your parents.
- You already know what to expect.

CONS

- Potential conflicts with parents if you change your mind or don't do well.
- Makes it hard to form your own identity.
- Feelings of guilt if you decide to leave the field.

■ My education prepared me to be a ...

Often, educational choices lead you directly to a career decision. For example, if you studied electrical engineering, it would seem logical to become an electrical engineer.

PROS

- The education prepares you for the career.
- You are likely to progress faster initially in your career.
- It places you in daily contact with others who have similar backgrounds.

CONS

- If you don't like the work, it can be a great disappointment.
- A gap often exists between what you expect and what you actually do.
- Many people have limited actual experience in the career and can easily make a bad choice.

■ Picking a job based on pay

Many experts suggest that you opt for higher-paying jobs when possible. This criterion is frequently important to young people and often remains so for experienced workers.

PROS

- High pay offers financial freedom and a comfortable lifestyle.
- Financial success can help you feel better about yourself.
- Such jobs often provide social status and recognition.

CONS

- An overemphasis on money can undermine your values and self-worth.
- Money can encourage unethical behavior and false friends.
- It may restrict you from seeking a more satisfying career, one that better matches your interests.

■ Seeking a job with high status

Some people want a job that "sounds good" or impresses others. If you are impressed by important-sounding job titles, you may be encouraged to seek this type of job.

PROS

- Such jobs may provide personal satisfaction.
- Others tend to view you as important, and this can enhance your social position.
- Such jobs often offer perks such as trips, cars, and free tickets to events.

CONS

- Some high-status jobs do not pay well.
- High-profile jobs often expose you to public criticism.
- Selecting a career on this basis alone may keep you from one that matches your true aspirations.

■ Based on information from a "career day"

More schools, universities, businesses, and government groups are now sponsoring career days. These events provide presentations on selecting a career, job seeking, resumes, and related topics. During career days, employers frequently recruit, provide information, and conduct initial interviews.

PROS

- You can learn about careers and meet employers without making a commitment.
- A wide variety of occupations is usually presented.
- It is a unique opportunity to ask questions and gather good information.

CONS

- You won't get much individual attention.
- The topics covered are general rather than specific to your situation.
- The information is often presented too quickly.

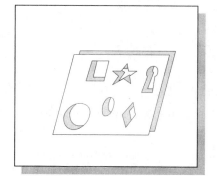

■ Relying on assessment tests

Various tests can help identify your personality traits, interests, or abilities and match them with those required for various jobs.

PROS

- Can save research time.
- Often reinforces your existing opinions or preferences.
- May introduce you to previously unconsidered options.

CONS

- Results can sometimes be superficial.
- Test results are easily misunderstood and may lead to wrong conclusions.
- Recommendations may not relate well to a rapidly changing work environment.

■ Based on information from computer systems

The number and variety of computerized career assessment and information systems are growing. Some ask questions and then use the information acquired to recommend jobs you should consider. Others provide detailed information on jobs which interest you.

PROS

- Can be convenient and easy to use.
- Some programs provide an enormous amount of information.
- Can help clarify several career considerations and cross-reference them with jobs they best match.

CONS

- A computer won't take your motivation and dreams into account.
- Proposed jobs are often too conventional.
- Incorrect use of the program can lead to misleading conclusions.

■ Listening to professional advisors

A variety of professionals provide career counseling. Many possess good knowledge of the employment market and can help you define career directions.

PROS

- Career counselors can provide objective and independent recommendations.
- Professionals may be better able to evaluate your potential than you.
- They can help you identify strengths and improve self-esteem.

CONS

- Career advisors may be expensive.
- There is risk involved when trying to find a good counselor.
- Even if qualified, counselors cannot be familiar with every type of job.

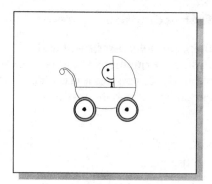

■ You are born knowing your destiny

Some fortunate people seem to know what they want to do almost from birth. Even when very young, they dream of having a specific vocation — and they go on to do it!

PROS

- Wonderfully easy decision-making.
- Often accompanied by substantial self-confidence.
- Concentration of energy and effort.

CONS

- You may miss out on more diverse experiences.
- If you fail, you can suffer a loss of direction.
- Extreme specialization results in a lack of versatility.

■ Working a variety of short-term jobs

Some people work in a variety of jobs for short periods of time. They may work for temporary agencies or simply change jobs frequently. This approach lets them try out many different jobs without major professional risk.

PROS

- Results in wide and diversified professional experiences.
- Can be a good way to test job interests.
- Can help avoid major career errors by eliminating jobs which don't suit you.

CONS

- This approach takes a long time before the "right" job is found.
- On-the-job experience is often limited.
- Can result in an employer viewing you as unreliable.

■ The hot jobs approach

Magazines and books often advise on current career trends, the best careers, the jobs of tomorrow.... They suggest that merely following their advice will land you the ideal job.

PROS

- They reveal the fastest-growing jobs and other advantages in the job market.
- They encourage you to consider jobs with good pay.
- Their advice is often reasonable and encourages you to make good choices.

CONS

- The approach promotes conformity in your job selection.
- You are not encouraged to define or follow your personal interests.
- Their advice may lead you to misuse your talents and enthusiasm.

■ Advice from friends and relatives

Your friends and relatives feel they know you well and frequently try to help by giving you advice based on their own experiences.

PROS

- They are a good source of strong personal support.
- Their advice is usually based on good common sense.
- Recommendations are spontaneous and sincere.

CONS

- Their advice may influence you too strongly.
- Situation may encourage you to be too passive in your job search.
- Relations may become strained if things go badly.

■ Job selection based on hobbies and recreational activities

Some fortunate people are able to turn a hobby or leisure activity into a full-time job.

This is an appealing option for many of us.

PROS

- Your choice will quickly make sense to others.
- You are almost assured of having a strong interest in your work.
- You are more likely to remain enthusiastic, even during boring tasks.

CONS

- The work may not pay well.
- You will often have to learn on the job rather than through formal training.
- There are usually few formal job options or opportunities for diversification.

■ Using internships and apprenticeships to make a decision

There are a variety of formal and informal ways to learn while you work. Apprenticeships mix classroom training with supervised on-the-job experience and can last from six months to several years. Internships, which normally operate on a volunteer basis, give you work experience related to your field and are usually available through schools. An internship offers an excellent chance to help you decide which career to choose.

PROS

- Furnishes contact with the real world of work.
- Provides a good basis for your career decision.
- Imparts firsthand knowledge of an organization.

CONS

- Good internships and apprenticeships can be hard to find.
- Low or no pay, particularly at the beginning.
- Time-consuming process.

■ Advice from those with whom you work

Coworkers and professional acquaintances are an unlimited source of ideas and inspiration. Their influence on your professional life is important. Many people take a job and work their way up, depending on the advice of those they work with to help them achieve success.

PROS

- Simple and direct approach.
- Allows you to develop talents and competencies similar to those needed in your present job.
- You possess knowledge of the field and job.

CONS

- The available jobs within the organization or field may not suit you.
- Training may be required to advance.
- The organization itself may not be a good choice.

■ Allowing parents to influence career decisions.

Through an excess of love and care, some parents push their children toward a particular career.

PROS

- This is an easy way to make a choice.
- Parents are likely to provide financial help and moral support.
- May be necessary if preparing to run a family business.

CONS

- You avoid responsibility for your own decision and creating your own identity.
- Your preferences and motivations may not be considered.
- Frustration with choice can lead to depression.

Presented below are the different methods described in this chapter. Review the methods and determine how useful each one would be (or has been) for making career decisions. Have fun!

Circle the box	If the method appeals to you	Or if you have used this method
– –	hardly at all	never
–	a little	rarely
+	some	sometimes
+ +	very much	often

Method #1

| – – | – | + | + + |

Method #2
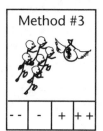

| – – | – | + | + + |

Method #3
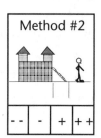

| – – | – | + | + + |

Method #4
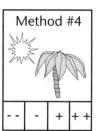

| – – | – | + | + + |

Method #5

| – – | – | + | + + |

Method #6
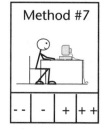

| – – | – | + | + + |

Method #7

| – – | – | + | + + |

Method #8

| – – | – | + | + + |

Method #9
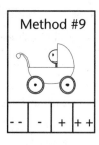

| – – | – | + | + + |

Method #10

| – – | – | + | + + |

Method #11

| – – | – | + | + + |

Method #12
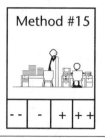

| – – | – | + | + + |

Method #13
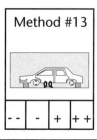

| – – | – | + | + + |

Method #14

| – – | – | + | + + |

Method #15
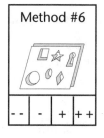

| – – | – | + | + + |

Method #16

| – – | – | + | + + |

The 16 methods which have been described to you have 2 significant drawbacks. They do not take into account:

> ➤ your aspirations or
> ➤ the job market.

Your Aspirations Are Essential!

The key to having a successful career is to do a job that corresponds to your interests. A job that inspires you. A job to which you can really commit yourself. A job in which you work with all your heart. A job that excites you. A job that utilizes your talents. A job that helps you grow. A job in which your work is respected. A job that offers recognition.

Knowledge of the Job Market also Is Essential!

It is essential to your career success to find a field that offers good employment opportunities. Therefore, it is important that you research the job market, career fields, and specific organizations so that you know where to invest your individual skills and talents. Then, the combination of your talents and opportunities of the market should be a successful match.

To combine your interests with the job market is a process that is both:

> ➤ difficult and
> ➤ complex.

Difficult because ...
> ➤ the stakes are of prime importance, and the techniques that exist today are rather unsophisticated;
> ➤ your decision is often made during times of desperation, rejection, or depression; and
> ➤ you are often faced with confusing choices because your priorities are not well-defined.

Complex because ...
> ➤ the words used by others when discussing employment and careers often have several meanings, and you may be confused about what is actually meant.

Therefore, when one talks about:

- ➤ **employment**
- ➤ **function**
- ➤ **field**
- ➤ **industry**
- ➤ **title**
- ➤ **career**
- ➤ **job**

nothing seems consistent or certain.

So many words, so much confusion!

So many people, so many concepts!

So many dictionaries, so many definitions!

To make things clearer and find some peace, you need to clarify things for yourself. This book is an invitation to identify your strengths, desires, and aptitudes, and define the values which are most important to you.

No one else can do this for you. If you don't do it, it will not get done!

2

THE KEY CRITERIA FOR YOUR NEXT JOB

Today, traditional job search paths are not sufficient to ensure that you will get a job tailored specifically to you. If, however, you are looking for a job which best uses your talents, then follow this guide.

The Key Criteria for Your Next Job

Talents

First of all, your talents will help you define your ideal title.

These are criteria that will describe your personal way of doing tasks.

In this book, a cap is used to illustrate your future title.

Therefore, if you like to:

- analyze
- compile
- compare

you possess the talents
of an **ACCOUNTANT.**

- listen
- convince
- demonstrate

you may consider
becoming a **TEACHER.**

- negotiate
- compare
- research

you may want to
be a **BUYER.**

Fields of Interest Which Inspire You

Those fields of interest that inspire you also help define your ideal field.

These are criteria that have less to do with you personally, and more to do with the outside world.

In this book, an oval area symbolizes your ideal field.

Therefore, if you like:

- basic natural elements

CHEMISTRY may attract you.

- food

COOKING
may seduce you.

- funiture

INTERIOR DECORATING
may suit you.

People with Whom You Want to Work

The Importance of Others to Your Career Success

If one excludes downsizing for economic reasons, four out of every five firings or dismissals result from:

> ➤ nonfunctional personal relationships, or

> ➤ working conditions that don't suit the person

with:

> ➤ bosses

> ➤ colleagues

> ➤ subordinates

> ➤ people external to your organization with whom you are in contact (accountants, suppliers, customers, etc.)

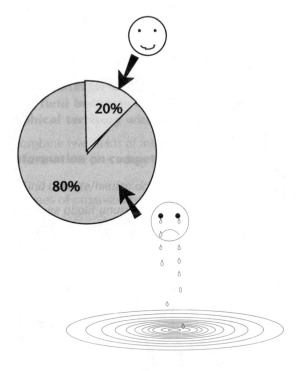

The Importance of Others to Your Career Success

The characteristics of people with whom you work can be these:

■ Intangible

I want to work with people who

> ➤ are to the point
> ➤ have a good sense of humor
> ➤ are sharp

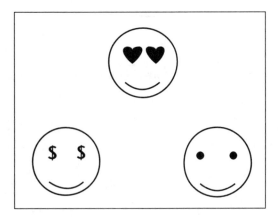

■ Tangible

and who are

> ➤ neat
> ➤ punctual
> ➤ reliable

The Four Types of People You Meet in Your Job

In every job, there are always four types of people around you:

➤ bosses

➤ colleagues

➤ subordinates

➤ external contacts (for example, customers for salespeople, students for teachers, …)

To identify the people you want to work with, complete the following two exercises.

Exercise #1

Classify, by order of decreasing importance (starting with the most important and ending with the least important), each one of the four types of people you are in contact with through your job.

Rank the type of people who are most important to you in your job as number one, rank the next most important people in your job as number two, etc., until the four boxes are filled.

BOSS RANK # _____	**COLLEAGUES** RANK # _____	**SUBORDINATES** RANK # _____	**EXTERNAL CONTACTS** RANK # _____

Different Personality Traits

Exercise # 2

Jot down between 15 and 30 personality traits that you dislike in the people with whom you work. List personality traits such as aggressive, rigid, vulgar, sad..., as well as negative characteristics such as unreliable, dirty, noisy, etc. Include those that affect you most or have a negative impact on your work.

❑ _____ ❑ _____ ❑ _____

❑ _____ ❑ _____ ❑ _____

❑ _____ ❑ _____ ❑ _____

❑ _____ ❑ _____ ❑ _____

❑ _____ ❑ _____ ❑ _____

❑ _____ ❑ _____ ❑ _____

❑ _____ ❑ _____ ❑ _____

❑ _____ ❑ _____ ❑ _____

❑ _____ ❑ _____ ❑ _____

❑ _____ ❑ _____ ❑ _____

❑ _____ ❑ _____ ❑ _____

❑ _____ ❑ _____ ❑ _____

❑ _____ ❑ _____ ❑ _____

❑ _____ ❑ _____ ❑ _____

Different Personality Traits (continued)

From all of the negative characteristics that you jotted down, circle the five that bother you the most.

Then, identify the antonym for each one of these five negative characteristics.

The antonym is often the opposite meaning of a word or the "positive" of the "negative."

For example:

stubborn	--------------------➤	flexible
greedy	--------------------➤	generous
late	--------------------➤	punctual
sad	--------------------➤	happy
deceitful	--------------------➤	honest
slow	--------------------➤	fast
moody	--------------------➤	pleasant
narrow-minded	--------------------➤	visionary

Write down each of the five antonyms in the square below.

If you have trouble identifying the antonyms, use a good thesaurus.

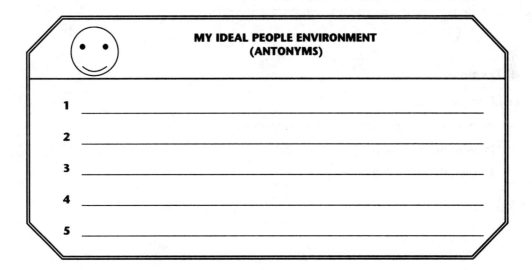

MY IDEAL PEOPLE ENVIRONMENT
(ANTONYMS)

1 _____

2 _____

3 _____

4 _____

5 _____

Pleasant Working Conditions

The working conditions that appeal to you offer essential criteria for choosing your next job. These working conditions can be tangible or intangible.

■ Intangible

I wish to get a job:

➤ that involves a lot of travel

➤ with a company that is on the leading edge

➤ with flex time

■ Tangible

I wish to get a job:

➤ where I can grow plants in my workspace

➤ with my own office

➤ with the latest computer software

Pleasant Working Conditions (continued)

To guarantee some stability in your job and, more importantly, to ensure professional growth, you must define five working conditions essential to you.

Below, write down all the working conditions you prefer. Jot down those that best help you succeed and thrive in your job.

Example: *medium-sized company*
clearly defined job objectives

❏ _____

❏ _____

❏ _____

❏ _____

❏ _____

❏ _____

❏ _____

❏ _____

❏ _____

❏ _____

❏ _____

❏ _____

❏ _____

❏ _____

❏ _____

❏ _____

❏ _____

❏ _____

Pleasant Working Conditions (continued)

On the list you just created, check the box next to the five working conditions that you consider to be the most important to ensuring success in your next job.

Write these on the following lines.

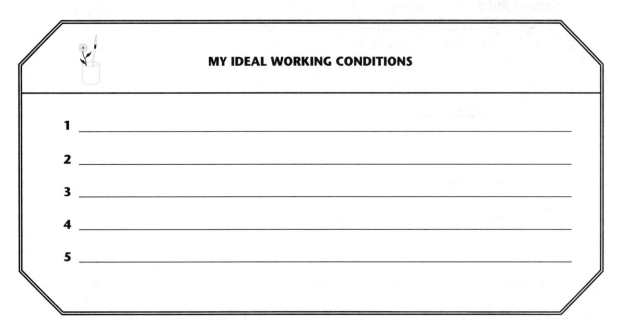

MY IDEAL WORKING CONDITIONS

1 _____

2 _____

3 _____

4 _____

5 _____

Unpleasant working conditions and the inability to get along with those you work with are the two major causes of job dissatisfaction.

> Keep in mind that four out of five dismissals or firings come from one of these two sources. Therefore, only one of every five dismissals or firings are due to a lack of competency or knowledge.

Identifying the kind of people with whom you want to work and the type of conditions you want to work in won't be sufficient to define your target job, but it will help you to:

➤ ask relevant questions during interviews so that you know which company best suits you.

➤ choose the best position from two or three job offers (by matching your expectations with the offers you receive).

Your Preferred Geographical Location

For many job seekers, geographical location is an important criterion when looking for a job. Therefore, it is important to address this aspect.

The main factors that frequently determine geographical area are:

> ➤ emotional reasons;
>
> ➤ cost of living;
>
> ➤ social opportunities;
>
> ➤ presence of friends or relationships;
>
> ➤ cultural events;
>
> ➤ educational possibilities for children; and
>
> ➤ proximity of hobbies.

In order to remain in a specific geographical area, you may have to make many sacrifices in your career. Some job possibilities may be eliminated because of this criterion.

Experience shows that geographical preferences often generate radical positions. Many irrational decisions are justified by seemingly good reasons …

In this area, some rationality won't hurt!

> One way to decide whether to accept or decline a job offer is to visit the place where the position is located. Another way is to discuss job opportunities with at least three people who work or have worked in the area.

Then, and only then, make your decision….

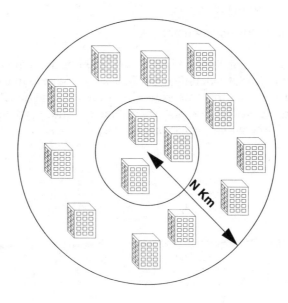

Other Criteria to Consider

There are many other criteria that affect the choice of the organization in which you want to work. Certain criteria will count more (or less) at different times in your career.

These criteria help narrow down, within your preferred geographical area, the list of organizations you have identified and want to approach.

■ The most frequently used criteria when choosing an organization are these:

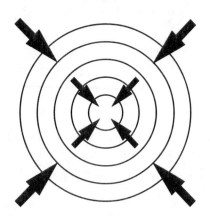

- rank in the industry
- number of employees
- turnover rate
- growth potential
- prestige
- status
- profitability
- structure
- scope (local/national/international)

■ Other criteria sometimes used have little relevance to the job:
- date of creation
- type of legal entity

■ Finally, an organization's "values" are often taken into account when a career decision is made, such as its:
- social conscience
- affirmative action policies
- protection of the environment, etc.

Unlike the previous criteria listed, these "values" cannot be found in company guides or annual reports. They are difficult to identify or verify. You will be able to evaluate these criteria only after you visit the organizations that interest you and spend some time talking about your specific interests with people who work there. These "values" criteria are useful and essential when you make your final choice among several job offers.

Other Criteria to Consider (continued)

MY SEVEN "VALUES" CRITERIA

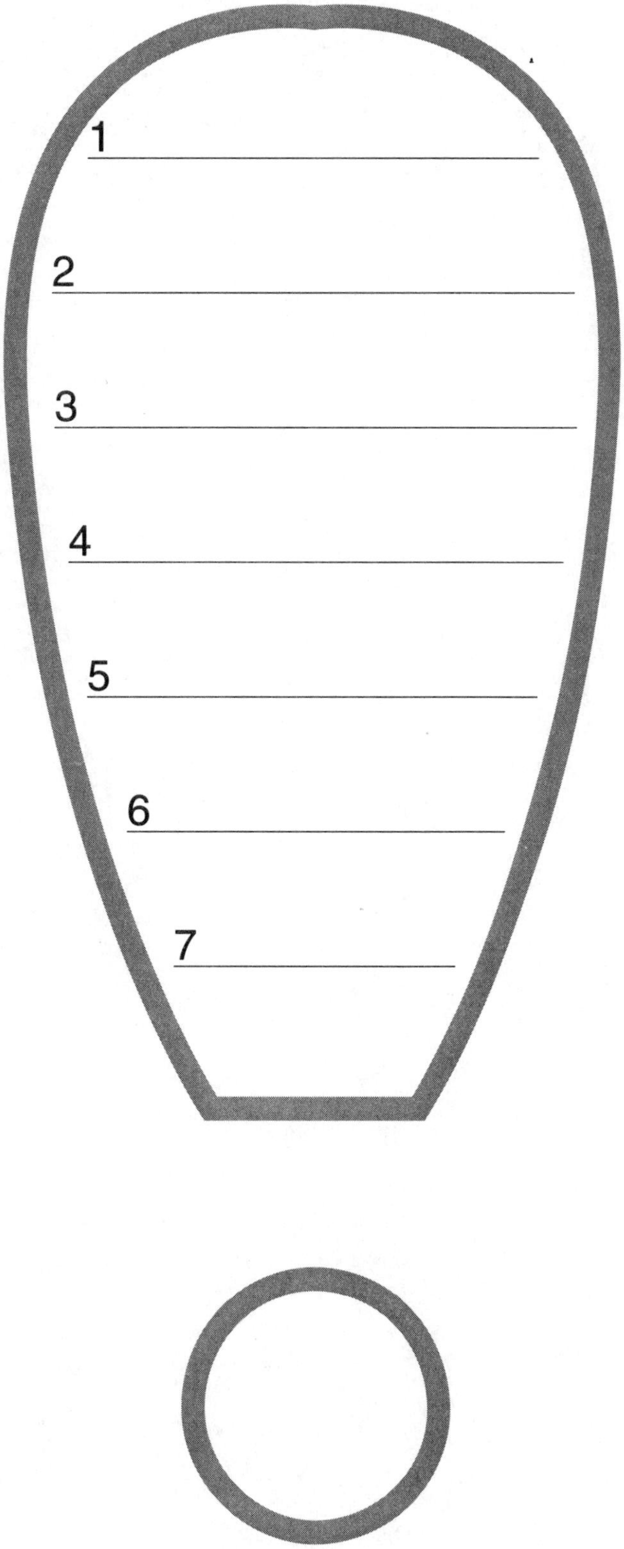

1 _____

2 _____

3 _____

4 _____

5 _____

6 _____

7 _____

3

THE TWO KEY COMPONENTS OF YOUR JOB: TITLE AND FIELD

Now that you know yourself better, you might have a better idea as to which type of career attracts you. In order to turn your career aspirations into a job, you must clarify the concepts of title (function) and field (industry).

The Two Key Components of Your Job: Title and Field

Definitions

As in many areas, the words you use when you discuss careers and jobs can cause confusion.

In job hunting, three words generate the greatest part of this confusion:

- ➤ **Title** (or function);
- ➤ **Field** (or industry); and
- ➤ **Job**.

To help clarify this area, here are three definitions:

- ➤ **The title** is the concentration of your talents in an area in which they thrive.
- ➤ **The field** is a branch of activity on which your preferred interests are centered.
- ➤ **The job** is your ideal **title** in the **field** which attracts you most.

Therefore, in this book, we understand a job to be the combination:

OF TITLE	**WITH FIELD**
(what you do)	(where you do it)

For example:

➤ a researcher	in the science field
➤ an accountant	in the clothing industry
➤ a controller	in the pharmaceutical field
➤ a salesperson	in the furniture industry
➤ a financier	in the field of technology
➤ an editor	in the publishing field
➤ a cook	in the tourism industry

Building Your Ideal Job: Title and Field

To identify your ideal job, you must be able to answer two key questions:

1. What is the name of the field that inspires you?

2. What is the name of the title that most attracts you?

You can take two different avenues to do this successfully:

1. Define the field first, then the title.

"I want to work in the **food industry** and be... "

"I want to work in the **furniture industry** and be... "

"I want to work in the **pharmaceutical industry** and be... "

Building Your Ideal Job: Field and Title

2. Define the title first, then the field.

"I want to be an **accountant** and work in… "

"I want to be an **editor** and work in… "

"I want to be a **buyer** and work in… "

■ Which avenue should you choose?

The majority of people follow the **second avenue**; they define the title first, then the field. This way seems more reasonable but actually generates a lot of career dissatisfaction. The reason for this is that nothing forces an employer to use a specific term for a particular job. One hundred different people might call themselves a "sales manager" and literally do 100 different jobs.

Avenue 1 seems less reasonable, and fewer people follow it. However, this avenue is closer to your heart and aspirations. Experience shows that it is a safer and more certain route.

Building Your Ideal Job: Field and Title (continued)

In the first case, you can choose:

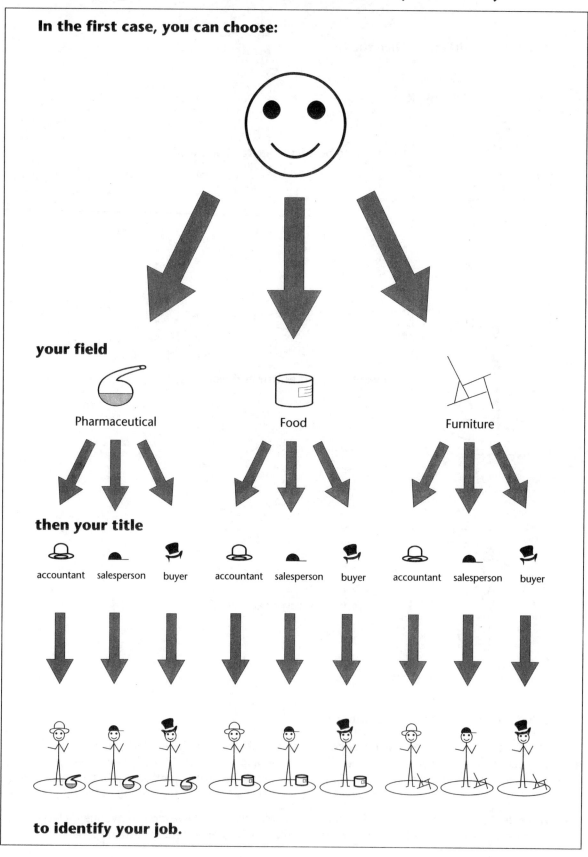

your field

Pharmaceutical   Food   Furniture

then your title

accountant   salesperson   buyer   accountant   salesperson   buyer   accountant   salesperson   buyer

to identify your job.

Building Your Ideal Job: Field and Title (continued)

In the second case, you can choose:

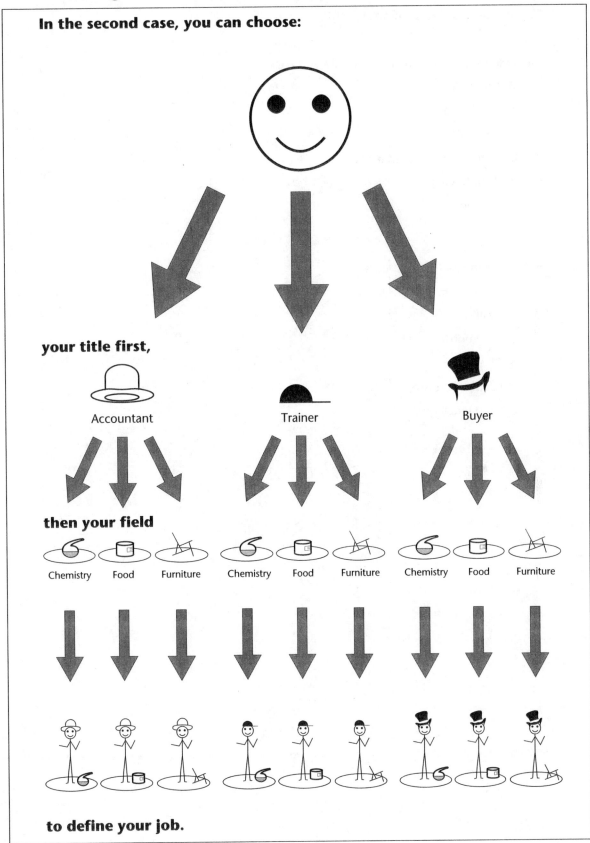

your title first,

Accountant   Trainer   Buyer

then your field

Chemistry Food Furniture Chemistry Food Furniture Chemistry Food Furniture

to define your job.

Building Your Ideal Job: Field and Title (continued)

To illustrate these ideas, complete this example.

Let's assume that the **titles** that inspire you are:

     A   Controller

     B   Salesperson

     C   Public Relations Specialist

     D   Human Resources Manager

     E   Plant Manager

     F   Accountant

and the **fields** that attract you are:

     1   Health Care

     2   Aviation

     3   Automobile

     4   Chemistry

     5   Building Industry

     6   Food Industry

Building Your Ideal Job: Field and Title (continued)

Combining these six titles with the six fields generates 36 combinations:

A1   Controller in Health Care

A2   Controller in Aviation

A3   Controller in Automobile Industry

A4   Controller in Chemistry

A5   Controller in Building Industry

A6   Controller in Food Industry

B1   Salesperson in Health Care

B2   Salesperson in Aviation

B3   Salesperson in Automobile Industry

B4   Salesperson in Chemistry

B5   Salesperson in Building Industry

B6   Salesperson in Food Industry

C1   Public Relations in Health Care

C2   Public Relations in Aviation

C3   Public Relations in Automobile Industry

C4   Public Relations in Chemistry

C5   Public Relations in Building Industry

C6   Public Relations in Food Industry

D1   Human Resources Manager in Health Care

D2   Human Resources Manager in Aviation

D3   Human Resources Manager in Automobile Industry

D4   Human Resources Manager in Chemistry

D5   Human Resources Manager in Building Industry

D6   Human Resources Manager in Food Industry

E1   Plant Manager in Health Care

E2   Plant Manager in Aviation

E3   Plant Manager in Automobile Industry

E4   Plant Manager in Chemistry

E5   Plant Manager in Building Industry

E6   Plant Manager in Food Industry

F1   Accountant in Health Care

F2   Accountant in Aviation

F3   Accountant in Automobile

F4   Accounant in Chemistry

F5   Accountant in Building Industry

F6   Accountant in Food Industry

You have many choices!!!

Evolution of Your Career and Change in Your Job

Depending on the importance that you place on your preferred criteria in a job, and how well you know your talents (transferable skills) and your preferred fields of interest, you can change one or both key parameters of your job.

You can, during the course of your career modify or radically change:

➤ your title; and

➤ your field.

Here are a few illustrations.

■ You can change your title and stay in the same field.

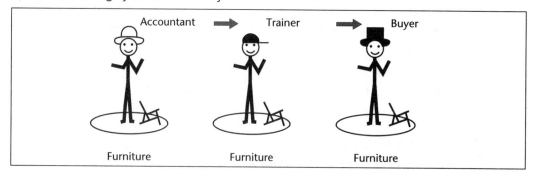

■ You can change fields and keep the same title.

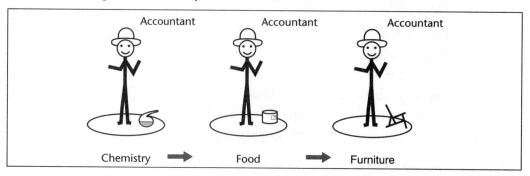

■ You can change both at the same time, field and title.

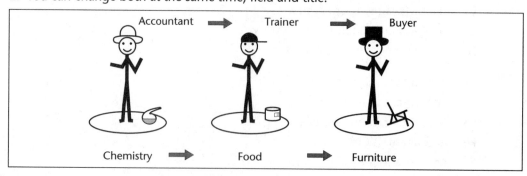

4

YOUR IDEAL TITLE: CROSSROADS OF YOUR TALENTS

If you understand what has been presented on the previous pages, you can already apply for a number of jobs. But take your time and proceed carefully. Learn how to identify the true responsibilities behind a title.

Your Ideal Title: Crossroads of Your Talents

The Ingredients of Your Job Function

Your job function is designated by the title.

Here are three examples of titles:

TITLE Product Manager of Marketing

TITLE Controller

TITLE Management Assistant

Defining Your Job Title: Difficult and Risky

Every title is associated with specific tasks (generally 15-25 tasks for any given title).

For example, here are three tasks for each of the titles listed on the preceding page.

Title	Product Manager In Marketing
Tasks	➤ Recommends marketing objectives
	➤ Suggests ideas for the development of new products
	➤ Gathers information on competitors' sales forces

Title	Controller
Tasks	➤ Coordinates the implementation of internal audit system
	➤ Identifies sources of errors
	➤ Suggests necessary steps to improve internal control

Title	Management Assistant
Tasks	➤ Prepares the shareholders' and board of directors' meetings
	➤ Establishes the agenda of the meetings
	➤ Follows legal rules (in investigations, proceedings, and other administrative procedures)

Discovering Your Talents

Often, a job title does not offer much information. At worst, it is the source of a lot of confusion and frustration. What a title means to you (the candidate), may mean something entirely different to someone else (the employer).

Hence, false agreements, frequent misunderstandings, and unfulfilled expectations exist on both sides... and clash!

The following examples illustrate this kind of confusion.

Identical titles, different tasks

In organizations within the same field, two identical titles can have entirely different tasks and responsibilities.

organization / title	A	B
Trainer	– training – selling workshops	– training only
Receptionist	– type correspondence to provide information	– no typing
Controller	– make recommendations – make some decisions – profitability	– make recommendations only

Identical titles, different tasks (continued)

Here is a comprehensive list of tasks performed by a trainer as they appear in the job descriptions of three organizations: A, B, C.

YES = ☑
NO = ☐

		Org A	Org B	Org C
1.	Identify needs	☑	☐	☑
2.	Plan seminars	☐	☑	☑
3.	Compile documents	☑	☑	☑
4.	Prepare transparencies	☑	☐	☑
5.	Devise tests	☐	☐	☑
6.	Define participant profiles	☑	☑	☑
7.	Recruit candidates	☐	☑	☐
8.	Raise funds	☐	☑	☐
9.	Organize logistics	☑	☑	☑
10.	Identify outside speakers	☐	☑	☐
11.	Establish a budget	☐	☑	☐
12.	Develop flyers	☐	☐	☑
13.	Confirm workshop registrations	☐	☑	☑
14.	Select venues	☐	☑	☐
15.	Open the workshop and perform the ice-breaking	☑	☑	☑
16.	Put participants at ease	☑	☑	☑
17.	Ensure workshop agenda is observed	☑	☑	☑
18.	Recommend readings	☐	☑	☑
19.	Train in different sites	☐	☑	☐
20.	Explain difficult concepts	☑	☑	☑
21.	Encourage participants	☑	☑	☑
22.	Attain objectives	☑	☑	☑
23.	Handle conflicts	☑	☑	☑
24.	Organize teams	☑	☑	☑
25.	Evaluate outside speakers	☐	☑	☐
26.	Hand out certificates of achievement	☐	☑	☑
27.	Verify that recommendations are implemented	☐	☑	☑
28.	Evaluate participants	☑	☑	☑
29.	Update programs	☐	☑	☑
30.	Create new workshops	☑	☑	☑
31.	Give consultation	☐	☐	☑
32.	Make strategic recommendations	☐	☑	☑

Different titles, identical tasks

Different titles can have very similar responsibilities. Never assume that you know a title's tasks. Always ask your potential employer to specify what duties are required of the person holding a particular title.

For instance:

➤ The titles "Internal Controller," "Internal Auditor," and "Financial Advisor" sometimes include identical tasks and responsibilities.

➤ Depending on the company, the title "Senior Executive" signals different levels of responsibility, which can be very different from each other.

➤ "Account Manager," "Manager Trainee," and "Account Executive" are titles that recruiters often use when they lack sales personnel and must use glamorous titles to attract employees.

These examples should warn you to be careful when considering job titles. To avoid mistakes, consider these recommendations.

Recommendation #1: Avoid limiting yourself to a title!

Never be satisfied with just a title. Be sure that you know the tasks and responsibilities attached to it.

Recommendation #2: Talk and listen!

Talk to people who actually hold the title that interests you. Ask them to describe the tasks associated with their title.

Recommendation #3: Ask for specifics!

Ask the interviewer what the title specifically includes in terms of tasks and responsibilities.

Different titles, identical tasks (continued)

The following examples illustrate the fact that organizations often assign different titles to the same tasks and responsibilities.

Tasks and responsibilities of *Associate Manager* for Maxifashion	Tasks and responsibilities of *Sales Advisor* for The StyleShop
Coordinating the shop Controlling inventory Handling inventory receipt and quality control Dressing windows Establishing selling prices Handling cash statements Handling daily statements Labeling Cleaning the shop Organizing the shop Reordering Making alterations Identifying needs Answering telephone calls Handling payments Billing and sales Checking invoices	Coordinating the shop Controlling inventory Handling inventory receipt and quality control Dressing windows Establishing selling prices Handling cash statements Handling daily statements Labeling Cleaning the shop Organizing the shop Reordering Making alterations Identifying needs Answering telephone calls Handling payments Billing and sales Checking invoices

Tasks and responsibilities of *Shop Manager* for Trends	Tasks and responsibilities of *Salesclerk* for FashionWorld
Coordinating the shop Controlling inventory Handling inventory receipt and quality control Dressing windows Establishing selling prices Handling cash statements Handling daily statements Labeling Cleaning the shop Organizing the shop Reordering Making alterations Identifying needs Answering telephone calls Handling payments Billing and sales Checking invoices	Coordinating the shop Controlling inventory Handling inventory receipt and quality control Dressing windows Establishing selling prices Handling cash statements Handling daily statements Labeling Cleaning the shop Organizing the shop Reordering Making alterations Identifying needs Answering telephone calls Handling payments Billing and sales Checking invoices

Suggestions for reducing both risk and difficulty

Never define a job solely by its title because it can be misleading and limiting. Titles are frequently interpreted in many different ways.

It is safer to describe a job in terms of its duties. Determine what tasks and responsibilities the job requires. Concentrate on what you can actually accomplish in the job.

Instead of locking yourself into a title, specify the responsibilities...

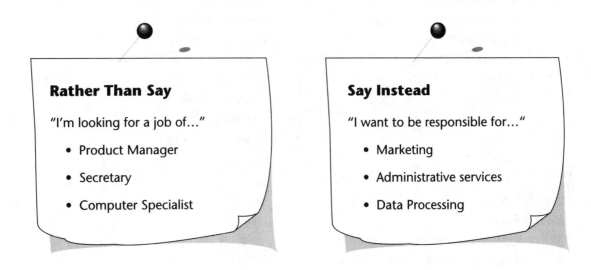

Rather Than Say

"I'm looking for a job of..."

- Product Manager
- Secretary
- Computer Specialist

Say Instead

"I want to be responsible for..."

- Marketing
- Administrative services
- Data Processing

To help prevent yourself from becoming locked into a job title, refer to the following list for examples of specific and general titles.

Suggestions for reducing both risk and difficulty (continued)

Titles	Equivalent Titles
Administrative Assistant	Secretary
Administrative Assistant	Receptionist
Administrative Assistant	Operations Assistant
Administrative Assistant	Office Support
Administrator	Profit Center Manager
Administrator	Division Manager
Administrator	General Manager
Administrator	Secretary
Auditor	Controller
Auditor	Financial Advisor
Auditor	Internal Auditor
Auditor	Financial Controller
Buyer	Acquirer
Buyer	Supplier
Buyer	Importer
Buyer	Negotiator
Customer Service Representative	Customer Relations
Customer Service Representative	Service Clerk
Customer Service Representative	Customer Support
Customer Service Representative	Receptionist
General Manager	Division Director
General Manager	Director of Membership
General Manager	Vice President
General Manager	Administrator
Marketing Representative	Salesperson
Marketing Representative	Product Manager
Marketing Representative	Telemarketer
Marketing Representative	Publicist
Personnel Director	Human Resources Director
Personnel Director	Recruiter
Personnel Director	Employee Relations Specialist
Personnel Director	Social Affairs Director
Public Relations Representative	Internal relations
Public Relations Representative	Media Relations
Public Relations Representative	International Relations
Public Relations Representative	Communications Director
Salesperson	Outside/Inside Sales
Salesperson	Accounts Manager
Salesperson	Closer
Salesperson	Manager Trainee

Talents

To carry out certain tasks, one must possess the needed talents (transferable skills).

For example:

Title   **Marketing Product Manager**

Task   ➤ **Recommend marketing objectives**

        Talents   *Estimate risks*

                   Evaluate implementation plans

                   Suggest new methods of accounting or pricing

                   Present ideas effectively

                   Etc.

Task   ➤ **Suggest ideas for the development of new products**

        Talents   *Create new products or services*

                   Devise simple solutions

                   Observe products on the market

                   Identify needs which are not satisfied

                   Work out plans of action

                   Etc.

Task   ➤ **Gather information on competitors' sales methods**

        Talents   *Find obscure/hidden data*

                   Inquire about unusual practices

                   Verify information

                   Compare approaches and methods

                   Speculate on intended purposes

                   Etc.

Talents (continued)

Title	Controller

Task ➤ **Coordinates the implementation of program for checking internal accounts**

       Talents   *Evaluate program proposals*

                       Measure impact of decisions

                       Control accounts

                       Coordinate practices

                       Ensure consistency within practices

                       Etc.

Task ➤ **Identify sources of mistakes**

       Talents   *Investigate practices*

                       Judge individuals and systems

                       Determine sources of error

                       Analyze complex situations

                       Evaluate the validity of statements

                       Etc.

Task ➤ **Suggest necessary modifications for implementing adequate internal control procedures**

       Talents   *Design control systems*

                       Simulate new practices

                       Structure complex procedures

                       Motivate people

                       Convince others of the usefulness of the methods

                       Etc.

Talents (continued)

Title	**Management Assistant**	
Task	➤ **Prepare shareholders' meetings**	
	Talents	*Organize details for meetings*
		Determine participants' expectations
		Identify company needs
		Plan events
		Solve problems
		Etc.
Task	➤ **Establish meeting minutes**	
	Talents	*Collect diversified information*
		Compile data
		Organize ideas, concepts
		Write reports
		Prioritize persuasive arguments
		Etc.
Task	➤ **Follow legal regulations (investigations, pursuits, and other administrative procedures)**	
	Talents	*Make inquiries about complex problems*
		Compare solutions for prompt decisions
		Organize meetings and reunions
		Stimulate programs
		Etc.

Defining Your Talents

To identify your ideal title, you must define the talents (transferable skills) that you enjoy using and want to apply in your next job. Ten to fifteen talents are sufficient for identifying a title.

According to a recent theory, anywhere between 12,000-15,000 different talents exist, and at birth, you are supposed to possess about 700 of them. In any given job, according to this theory, you utilize about 70 talents. This means that you only draw on about 10 percent of your potential.

A lengthy list of talents is provided on the following pages to assist you in identifying your transferable skills. Your objective is to identify 10 to 15 talents that you would like to use most in your next job. To identify these talents, follow four steps:

Step #1   Go through the list and add any talents that come to mind.

Step #2   Check all of your talents.

Step #3   Refer back to those talents you checked, and place a second check mark next to those you most prefer to use.

Step #4   Go over those talents you have checked twice, and place a third check mark next to the ones you favor... and so on until you end up with a list of 10 to 15 talents (transferable skills).

You should then be able to identify a title which corresponds to the talents you have selected.

There is nothing on today's market like a dictionary or thesaurus that provides a comprehensive list of talents and then names titles which correspond to them. Such a source is impossible to create because of the diversity of organizations and the rapid rate of change in the job market. It is only through trial and error that you will arrive at the name of your ideal job title. One of the most efficient methods to identify the name of this ideal job is the PIE Method. Its major advantage is that risks are limited because reliability is maximized. You will know what you are looking for. This makes you different from 99 percent of your competitors, who never take the time to figure out what it is they are looking for.

Defining Your Talents (continued)

Talents

Accommodating	Collaborating	Deciding	Establishing
Accomplishing	Collecting	Decorating	Evaluating
Achieving	Combining	Defending	Examining
Acquiring	Commanding	Defining	Experimenting
Activating	Communicating	Delegating	Explaining
Adapting	Competing	Delivering	Exploiting
Adding	Compiling	Demonstrating	Exporting
Addressing	Completing	Designing	Expressing
Administering	Composing	Detailing	Evoking
Admitting	Computing	Detecting	Facilitating
Adopting	Conceiving	Determining	Figuring
Advancing	Conceptualizing	Developing	Filing
Affirming	Concluding	Diagnosing	Financing
Analyzing	Condensing	Directing	Firing
Anticipating	Conferring	Discerning	Forming
Applying	Confiding	Discovering	Giving
Appraising	Confirming	Dispensing	Governing
Approving	Connecting	Distributing	Guaranteeing
Arbitrating	Conserving	Documenting	Guiding
Arranging	Consolidating	Drawing	Handling
Assembling	Consulting	Driving	Heading
Assisting	Contracting	Editing	Helping
Augmenting	Controlling	Educating	Hiring
Balancing	Coordinating	Elaborating	Identifying
Budgeting	Copying	Electing	Illustrating
Building	Correcting	Eliminating	Imagining
Buying	Correlating	Employing	Implementing
Calculating	Counseling	Engineering	Importing
Cataloging	Conversing	Enriching	Improving
Centralizing	Converting	Enrolling	Improvising
Choosing	Convincing	Enterprising	Inciting
Clarifying	Creating	Entertaining	Increasing
Classifying	Decentralizing	Estimating	Indexing

Defining Your Talents (continued)

Talents

Influencing	Perceiving	Recommending	Studying
Informing	Persevering	Reconciling	Suggesting
Initiating	Persuading	Recording	Summarizing
Inspecting	Photographing	Recruiting	Supervising
Installing	Planning	Rectifying	Surveying
Instructing	Predicting	Reducing	Synthesizing
Interpreting	Preparing	Refining	Systematizing
Intervening	Prescribing	Reforming	Testing
Interviewing	Presenting	Regulating	Thinking
Inventing	Presiding	Rehabilitating	Trading
Investigating	Preventing	Reinforcing	Training
Investing	Proceeding	Reorganizing	Transforming
Judging	Procuring	Repairing	Translating
Leading	Producing	Reporting	Transporting
Learning	Programming	Representing	Understanding
Liquidating	Projecting	Researching	Unifying
Maintaining	Promoting	Resolving	Uniting
Managing	Proofreading	Restructuring	Utilizing
Manipulating	Proposing	Revising	Updating
Maneuvering	Prospecting	Revitalizing	Verbalizing
Manufacturing	Protecting	Sanctioning	Verifying
Marketing	Providing	Sculpting	Wagering
Merging	Proving	Searching	Writing
Modeling	Publishing	Securing	
Moderating	Pursuing	Selling	
Motivating	Qualifying	Serving	
Navigating	Quantifying	Simplifying	
Negotiating	Questioning	Soliciting	
Observing	Raising	Solving	
Obtaining	Reading	Speaking	
Organizing	Realizing	Standardizing	
Originating	Reasoning	Stimulating	
Participating	Rebuilding	Structuring	

Defining Your Talents (continued)

In the box below, list the 10 to 15 talents (transferable skills) that you most want to use in your next job.

The Talents (Transferable Skills) That I Wish To Use in My Next Job		
1.	6.	11.
2.	7.	12.
3.	8.	13.
4.	9.	14.
5.	10.	15.

This list of talents may sound abstract because it is not always easy to relate your talents to a specific job. To ease this difficult process try to identify an objective which matches each of your talents. This will help ground your talents and make them less abstract. Then, on the next page, list your talents and the objectives which complement them.

Do not be too specific or too vague when identifying your objectives. The balance is not easy to find, but practice helps.

For example:

➤ Too specific…

  "I want to develop an electronic security system which should be installed near the kitchen to protect people in case of fire."

➤ Too vague…

  "I want to develop systems."

➤ Well-defined objective…

  "I wish to develop a security system which protects people in their daily lives."

Defining Your Talents (continued)

In the left-hand column, list the talents that you have identified; then list the complementary job objectives in the right-hand column.

Talents	Objectives
1.	
2.	
3.	
4.	
5.	
6.	
7.	
8.	
9.	
10.	
11.	
12.	
13.	
14.	
15.	

Examine your list of talents and job objectives. You may want to show your list to relatives and friends or consult job search books. It is preferable to survey people who actually work in fields that attract you and ask them how to identify jobs that utilize the talents on your list.

Surveying these professionals can provide hints as well as references to jobs and companies which are unfamiliar to you.

Defining Your Talents (continued)

After you have conducted your survey, record the names of six job titles that you have gathered that seem to match your preferred talents (transferable skills).

	Possible Job Titles **I want to be given responsibilities as a/an:**
1.	
2.	
3.	
4.	
5.	
6.	

5

YOUR PREFERRED FIELD: CROSSROADS OF YOUR INTERESTS

You have now defined your talents and discovered some of the interesting options and avenues which are open to you. The next step is to identify your preferred fields of interest.

Your Preferred Field: Crossroads of Your Interests

Characteristics of a Field

A field is sometimes referred to as an industry, branch, or sector.

One organization may belong to several fields:

> ➤ automobile
>
> ➤ aviation
>
> ➤ transportation
>
> ➤ health, etc.

To determine your ideal field or the industry in which you want to work, begin with your areas of interest.

For example:

> ➤ If you enjoy working with wood, you could seek employment in the wood industry.
>
> ➤ If designing machinery interests you, you might enjoy mechanical engineering.
>
> ➤ If clothing catches your eye, you may want to approach the fashion industry.

Some fields are extremely wide:

> ➤ education
>
> ➤ travel

Others are very narrow:

> ➤ preservation of human organs
>
> ➤ or underwear for infants

A wide field encompasses thousands of organizations, while a narrow field comprises a limited number of organizations (5-15).

The narrower the field, the easier it is to identify your target organization. For example, it is easier to gather information on companies that import meat to produce salami than it is to obtain information on organizations within the health industry.

Characteristics of a Field (continued)

The following three examples help illustrate how to narrow down a field.

Case # 1 David

David is fascinated by automobiles. In the *Yellow Pages*, he locates the geographic area where he wants to work and discovers 257 organizations for possible employment. Overwhelmed, David has no idea where to begin.

To narrow down the number of organizations in his field, David matches his primary field of interest (automobile) to three other fields of interest: finance, repair, and transportation.

Here are the results from combining David's fields of interest.

Automobile and Finance

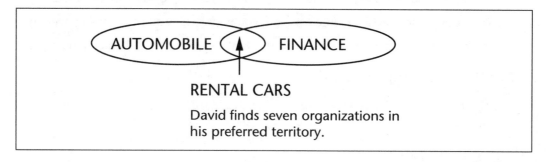

Automobile and Repair Shops

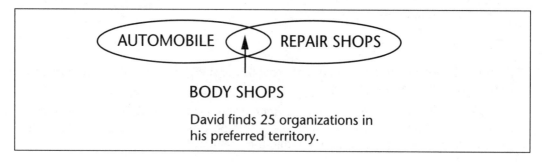

Automobile and Transportation

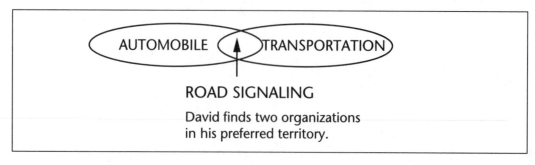

Characteristics of a Field (continued)

Case # 2 Michelle

Michelle has one passion in life: aviation.

But aviation is a huge field! More than 110 organizations are listed in the *Yellow Pages* of Michelle's telephone book in this area.

Michelle is attracted to three other fields too: meteorology, interior design, and cooking. Matching these fields with aviation helps clarify Michelle's preferred fields of interest.

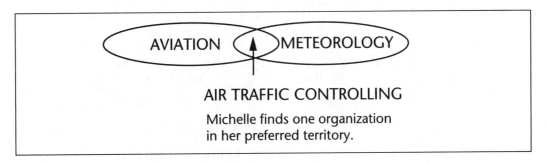

Aviation and Meteorology

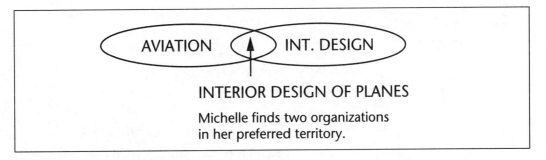

Aviation and Interior Design

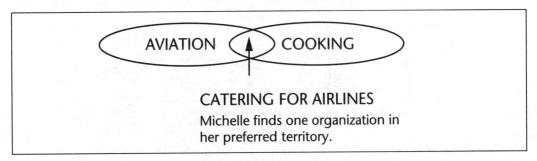

5.1 Characteristics of a Field (continued)

Case # 3 Lisa

Lisa adores music. Although she does not play an instrument, she is fascinated by the world of music.

Ninety-seven organizations are listed in the *Yellow Pages* under the heading "Music." First, Lisa is delighted to realize that she could work in 97 different places, but then she is discouraged by the number of options to explore.

In addition to music, three fields of interest attract Lisa: health, aviation, and travel. By combining her interests, Lisa has various options.

Music and Health

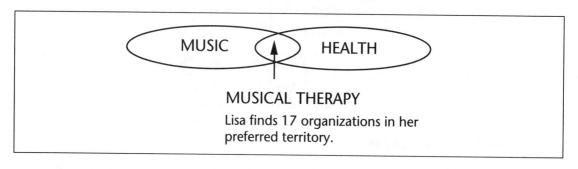

MUSICAL THERAPY
Lisa finds 17 organizations in her preferred territory.

Music and Aviation

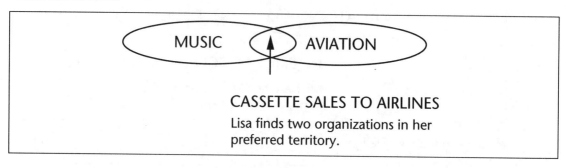

CASSETTE SALES TO AIRLINES
Lisa finds two organizations in her preferred territory.

Music and Travel

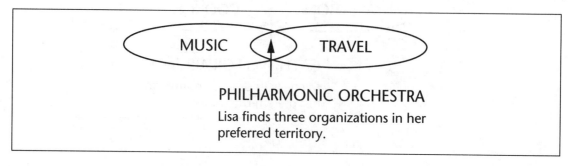

PHILHARMONIC ORCHESTRA
Lisa finds three organizations in her preferred territory.

Characteristics of a Field (continued)

Here is an example illustrating all the different fields of interest for a particular person. It specifies, for each one of the overlapping interests, the possible number of organizations found in the *Yellow Pages* of the area in which this person wants to work.

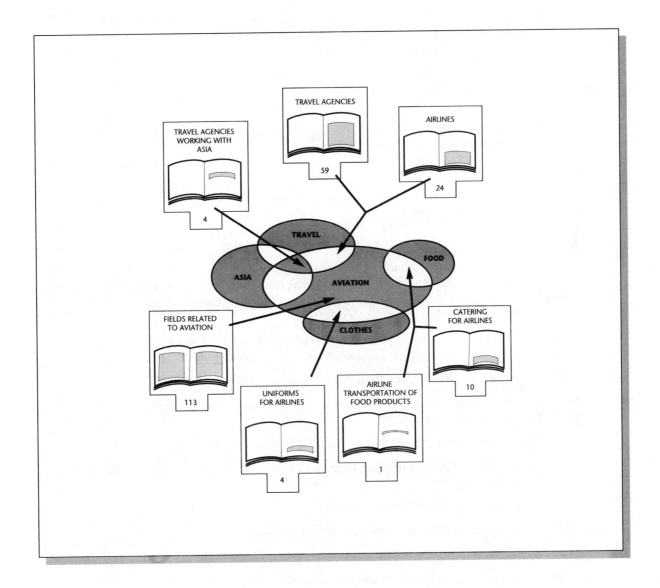

Choosing Your Field: Difficulties and Risks

To help make your search easier, the field you select should adhere to two rules.

Rule #1

The field should correspond to your interests, but it does not necessarily need to be an area in which you have a high level of expertise or experience.

Rule #2

Your field should be narrowly defined. It should be reduced until it includes from 5 to 15 organizations in the area where you want to work.

Choosing too safe a field

Surprisingly, your worst enemy in identifying your field is yourself.

When facing a career crisis or job uncertainty, people tend to look for jobs in fields that are safe or logical. Such a field may not excite or interest you, but you may feel comfortable in terms of expertise. During a crisis, fields that you know well frequently take precedence over those in which you'd prefer to work.

Ideally you should pick a field that you know and enjoy. However, do not hesitate to consider a field that inspires you, but in which you have little or no experience.

When choosing a field, listen to your heart rather than your head.

Why should you choose a field that inspires you? Quite simply because you should have a positive attitude toward your field.

➤ You will approach the job search enthusiastically and therefore land more interviews;

➤ You will be in a stronger position to negotiate your future job because you will be more relaxed and confident;

➤ You will integrate easily into organizations;

➤ You will more readily retain new things that you learn;

➤ You will be more efficient and productive; and

➤ You will connect well with people in your field and job.

The most common error you can make when choosing a field is to play it too safe.

Choosing too safe a field (continued)

To demonstrate that the field in which you work should interest you, take the following test.

If you have the choice between two job offers with the same title but in organizations belonging to different fields, which one would you choose? In the following examples, check the box of the field that you prefer.

1.   ❏   Luxury Products or
     ❏   Precision Mechanics

2.   ❏   Social Services or
     ❏   Technological Transfers

3.   ❏   Automotive or
     ❏   High Fashion

4.   ❏   Waste Water Treatment or
     ❏   Data Processing

5.   ❏   Chemical Products or
     ❏   Clothing

6.   ❏   Surgical Instruments or
     ❏   Construction

7.   ❏   Hotels or
     ❏   Camping Equipment

8.   ❏   Sports or
     ❏   Literature

9.   ❏   Electronics or
     ❏   Tourism

10. ❏   Publishing or
     ❏   Transportation

11. ❏   Coal Mining or
     ❏   Ship Building

12. ❏   Agriculture or
     ❏   Customer Service

13. ❏   Cutlery or
     ❏   Insurance

14. ❏   Steel or
     ❏   Banking

15. ❏   Department Stores or
     ❏   Art

16. ❏   Dry Cleaning or
     ❏   Investments

17. ❏   Fast Food or
     ❏   Luxury Products

18. ❏   Teaching or
     ❏   Tourism

Choosing too wide a field

The second most common error that people make when choosing a field is they fail to be specific enough.

People tend to select a wide field rather than a narrow one, assuming:

"The wider my field, the more opportunities I will have to find a job."

This contradicts everything we have learned in our work with thousands of job seekers and course participants.

The wider your field, the less chance you have of finding a job!

The opposite of what most people believe will happen occurs.

When searching for a job in a large field, you will not be able to communicate specifically enough. Your words and examples will be too general. Employers will perceive you as somebody who is "good for everything" but therefore "good for nothing."

When you interview in a wide field, the language you use is adapted so as to communicate with a large and diverse group of people. It is too universal and ineffective.

The graph on the next page shows what occurs during the average job search.

➤ In the beginning you usually look for a job identical to the one you just lost (A).

➤ If things do not work out quickly, you start to widen your target market (B, C, D).

➤ You end up with a target that is too wide (E).

➤ Then, you reassess and develop three new narrow targets (F1, F2, F3) and a "Plan B" (F4).

Choosing too wide a field (continued)

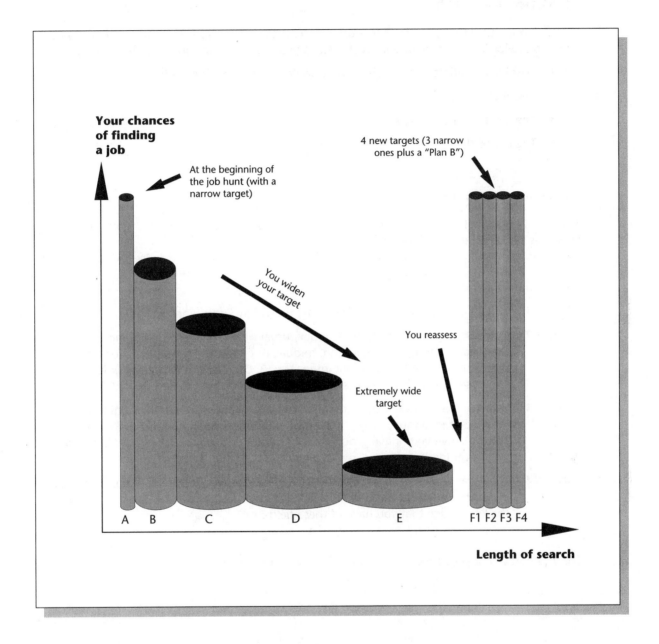

To successfully find a job in a field which excites you, you must identify your preferred areas of interest and jobs which most inspire you.

You do not have to be an expert in a certain field or even know it especially well. But you must be interested in the field or, even better, be passionate about it. The following pages should help you identify a specific field.

Discovering Your Fields of Interest

Identification methods

Identifying the field that you prefer to work in is actually quite simple. It means listening to your heart and following where your enthusiasm leads you. Listen to passion rather than reason.

Several possible identification methods exist, but we recommend these three:

➤ The *Yellow Pages*;

➤ The creative cards exercise; and

➤ The checklist.

The *Yellow Pages* method

The *Yellow Pages* method consists of identifying 5-15 fields of interest from the thousands of headings listed in the telephone book.

Proceed in four steps:

Step #1   Obtain a pink highlighter, a blue one, the *Yellow Pages*, and a pencil.

Step #2   Open the telephone book to its index, usually located at the beginning of the book. Start reading from the beginning, middle, or end of the list. Using your pink highlighter, mark any field that interests you. Do not worry about your level of expertise or knowledge in these fields! Highlight approximately 100-200 fields.

Step #3   When you are finished with step 2, go back over the fields you highlighted. Using your blue highlighter, mark those fields which inspire you the most. You should narrow down your initial group to 30-50 violet fields of interest (violet is pink and blue combined).

Step #4   Now that you have identified 30-50 fields, take a pencil and circle those 5-15 fields in which you would most like to work. Do not take into account your expertise or the knowledge that you have of these fields.

This method will help you successfully identify your "target fields."

The Yellow Pages (continued)

Sample from the *Yellow Pages*

Creative cards

The creative cards method uses 10 exercises.

On the following pages, you will find two exercises per page. For each exercise, jot down the fields of interest and subjects that inspire or attract you.

You should not exclusively list fields in which you have expertise but no excitement. But neither should you list only those fields which inspire you, but of which you have no knowledge.

You should identify at least 50 fields of interest and subjects in which you possess some knowledge and which inspire or attract you.

This may seem like a huge task, but these exercises are actually simpler and quicker than you might think.

Sometimes, the same fields of interest and subjects appear several times in each of these exercises. Do not worry about duplicates; you will eliminate them later.

Also, you do not have to fill out the cards in the order they appear. It is okay to skip any of those which do not interest you.

The ultimate goal of this exercise is to identify at least 50 fields of interest or subjects from the cards.

Good luck and have fun!

Creative cards (continued)

| **Game 1: The People** |

Here is a list of friends/people/acquaintances whom I know (taken from my address book).

They make me think of/we've talked about… (list all subjects that interest you both, professional and nonprofessional). When you spend time with each of these people, what do you talk about?

Examples:

William Bridgewater   theatre, architecture, fishing

| **Game 2: The Bookstore** |

If you were to spend an hour in a bookstore, or if you got locked in one for the weekend, what kinds of books would you look for? Books on which subjects would interest you? Make sure that you do not list types of books (for example, short novels, comics, etc.) but themes of books (for example, history, psychology, wildlife,…).

Examples:

Aviation

Optics

Marketing

Creative cards (continued)

Game 3: The Photo Album

Flip through your photo album. (If you do not keep a photo album, look through some magazines.) A number of photos will remind you of fields of interest which attract you. What are the fields that come to mind as you view the photos?

Examples:

Football _____   _____

Computers _____   _____

Woodworking _____   _____

_____   _____

_____   _____

_____   _____

_____   _____

_____   _____

Game 4: The Conference Center

If you (as you are clearly qualified to do) were appointed chief advisor to a huge conference center, what programs/topics/subjects would you recommend for a conference? You do not need to be knowledgeable about these subjects, only inspired by them.

Examples:

Graphic arts _____   _____

Electricity _____   _____

Birds _____   _____

_____   _____

_____   _____

_____   _____

_____   _____

_____   _____

Creative cards (continued)

| **Game 5: The Mail Catalogue** |

As usual (!) you don't have much to do. You decide to flip through the pages of a very thick mail order catalogue — the kind of catalogue in which you find anything and everything. On which pages would you spend the most time? You could also imagine that, coming back from a trip around the world, you find your mailbox loaded with highly specialized mail order catalogues. Of course you throw most of them away, but certain ones interest you enough to keep them. What types of catalogues are they?

Examples:

Gardening

Leather goods

Fishing

| **Game 6: The Mall** |

You are going to spend a few hours browsing through a huge mall. It is a super-maxi-jumbo mall in terms of its number of retail stores. Each retail store specializes in something: industrial goods, services, consumer goods, etc. Where do you stop to browse?

Examples:

Books

Tennis equipment

Furniture

Creative cards (continued)

| **Game 7: The Airport** |

During a trip, you are waiting in an airport for a connecting flight. Because of "the unexpected late arrival" of your plane, you have to wait another two and a half hours. You decide to head to the souvenir shop, and discover it has 2001 magazines. Which ones do you flip through?

Examples:

Sports _____ _____

Fashion _____ _____

Automotive _____ _____

_____ _____

_____ _____

_____ _____

_____ _____

| **Game 8: I've Got Nothing to Do** |

Assume that, because of unpredictable events, all that you had planned for the coming afternoon/day/weekend/week/month won't occur. What are you going to do now that you have nothing planned? List the fields/areas in which you'll be active. Use nouns rather than verbs.

Examples:

Gardens _____ _____

History _____ _____

Animals _____ _____

_____ _____

_____ _____

_____ _____

_____ _____

Creative cards (continued)

| **Game 9: The Trade Fairs** |

You are being offered 50 round-trip airline tickets along with tickets to 50 trade fairs and exhibitions. Which ones do you pick? These fairs need not exist, except in your imagination. Do not write the name of the town where they take place or their names; just list the topic or field they cover. It is okay to be specific — but not too specific!

Examples:

Communications _____   _____

Nature _____   _____

Paper trade _____   _____

_____   _____

_____   _____

_____   _____

_____   _____

_____   _____

| **Game 10: The Alien** |

An alien disembarks from its UFO and approaches you for help. It wants you to introduce/familiarize/acquaint it with some basic knowledge of the things/subjects/fields of interest that you know and enjoy (a lot or a little).

Examples:

Decorating _____   _____

Mathematics _____   _____

Mountains _____   _____

_____   _____

_____   _____

_____   _____

_____   _____

_____   _____

The checklist

┌─────────────────────────────────────┐
│   **Game 11: The Checklist**   │
└─────────────────────────────────────┘

Check off on this list the fields of interest/areas/topics which interest you, that you are enthusiastic about, and in which you have at least basic knowledge.

❑	Accounting	❑	Cooking
❑	Advertising	❑	Counseling
❑	Aerobics	❑	Customs
❑	Aeronautics	❑	Dance
❑	Aesthetics	❑	Data Processing
❑	Agriculture	❑	Decorating
❑	Analysis	❑	Dentistry
❑	Animals	❑	Designing
❑	Antiques	❑	Drafting
❑	Aquaculture	❑	Economics
❑	Architecture	❑	Editing
❑	Art	❑	Education
❑	Auditing	❑	Electricity
❑	Automobiles	❑	Electronics
❑	Banking	❑	Engineering
❑	Biology	❑	Farming
❑	Bookkeeping	❑	Fashion
❑	Broadcasting	❑	Finance
❑	Budgeting	❑	Fiscal Matters
❑	Building	❑	Foreign Languages
❑	Calculating	❑	Forestry
❑	Carpentry	❑	Fund-raising
❑	Chemistry	❑	Furniture
❑	Clothing	❑	Gardening
❑	Commerce	❑	Geology
❑	Communications	❑	Glass Works
❑	Community Affairs	❑	Government
❑	Computers	❑	Graphic Design
❑	Construction	❑	Hair Styling
❑	Consulting	❑	Handicrafts

The checklist (continued)

❏ Health	❏ Politics
❏ Hotel	❏ Printing
❏ Human Relations	❏ Production
❏ Imports-Exports	❏ Psychology
❏ Industry	❏ Public Relations
❏ Inspection	❏ Publishing
❏ Insurance	❏ Radio
❏ Investments	❏ Real Estate
❏ Jewelry Making	❏ Recycling
❏ Journalism	❏ Religion
❏ Landscaping	❏ Research
❏ Law	❏ Retail
❏ Machinery	❏ Rubber
❏ Maintenance	❏ Safety
❏ Marketing	❏ Sales
❏ Mechanics	❏ Security
❏ Medicine	❏ Social Sciences
❏ Metals	❏ Sports
❏ Meteorology	❏ Statistics
❏ Military	❏ Surveying
❏ Mining	❏ Television
❏ Music	❏ Textiles
❏ Natural Sciences	❏ Theatre
❏ Navigation	❏ Tourism
❏ Nursing	❏ Training
❏ Oceanography	❏ Transportation
❏ Painting	❏ Travel
❏ Paper Products	❏ Volunteering
❏ Performing Arts	❏ Waste Treatment
❏ Petroleum	❏ Welding
❏ Photography	❏ Woodworking
❏ Physical Therapy	❏ Writing
❏ Plastics	❏ Youth
❏ Plumbing	❏ Zoology
❏ Police	

Results

Compiling your discoveries

You have now identified at least 50 different fields of interest in the preceding exercises.

Divide these fields into the boxes of the square at the bottom of this page.

This allocation is completely subjective. If you can't decide where to place a field, put it aside and come back to it when you have placed the others.

If you find the choices too difficult, you could subdivide the enthusiasm or expertise section into three or four columns instead of two.

Here are some examples for completing the exercise:

➤ If *gardening really excites you, but you do not know much about the field, put it in box 2.*

➤ If *you like aviation and you know a lot about it, put it in box 3.*

➤ If *you love fishing and are an expert at it, put it in box 1.*

➤ If *navigation excites you a little and you know the basic principles of it, put it in box 4.*

	+ **Enthusiasm** low or average	**+++** **Enthusiasm** high or very high
+ **Expertise** low or average	(4)	(2)
+++ **Expertise** high or very high	(3)	(1)

Processing your discoveries

Now, locate the five fields which inspire you the most in the boxes on the preceding page. Pick these five from the fields you listed in box 1. If you do not have enough in that box, move on to box 2. If necessary, proceed to boxes 3 and 4.

On the following lines, write down the five fields that you selected.

My Preferred Fields

1.

2.

3.

4.

5.

Your preferred fields of interest will become operational when you define a narrow target field. A target field becomes narrow when no more than 5-15 organizations exist in the geographical territory where you want to work.

For this you have to combine two fields of interest to get the name of overlapping fields. An example was given to you on the preceding page. A table is also provided to aid in your research.

Finally, to determine names of organizations which correspond to your target fields, you can proceed down two different avenues:

➤ discuss your situation with friends, acquaintances, relatives, or colleagues. They will give you ideas and some names of organizations. This choice would be simple and productive; or

➤ consult telephone books or professional annuals. The *Yellow Pages* will give you multitudes of company names and addresses. This avenue would be more systematic and, therefore, more thorough.

Later, the section covering the PIE Method will explain in more detail how to utilize your friends and relatives without taking advantage of them.

Processing your discoveries (continued)

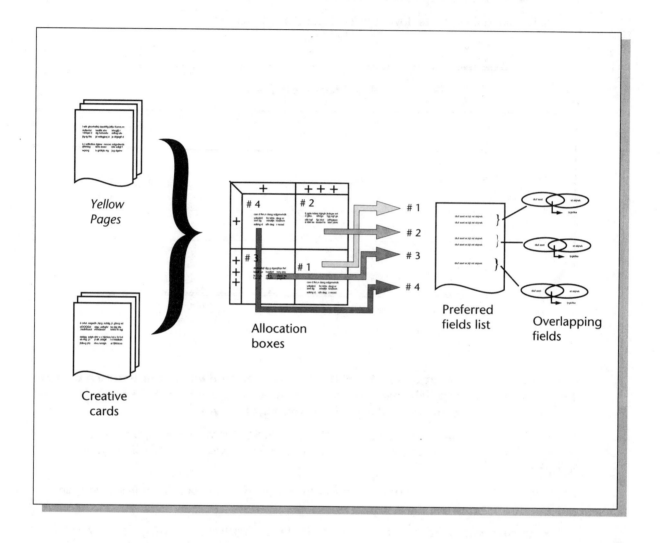

Yellow Pages

Creative cards

Allocation boxes

4   # 2   # 3   # 1

1   # 2   # 3   # 4

Preferred fields list

Overlapping fields

Processing your discoveries (continued)

Here is an example of someone who is interested in five fields: finance, automobile, food, tourism, and architecture.

She has listed each field twice:

> ➤ at the top of the columns (A, B, C,...); and

> ➤ at the side of the rows (1, 2, 3,...).

In each of the boxes (A1, B3, C2,...), she has listed the overlapping fields which result from combining the columns and rows.

For instance, if you combine tourism and architecture (D1) you get at least five specific fields: Office of Tourism, Urban Tourism, Promotion of Historic Buildings, Monument Preservation, and Publication of Tourist Guides.

	A	B	C	D	E
	FINANCE	**AUTOMOBILE**	**FOOD**	**TOURISM**	**ARCHITECTURE**
1 **ARCHITECTURE**	• Real Estate Insurance • Mortgages • Real Estate Promotion • Safe Manufacturing • Constructing Banks • Financing Tourism Projects	• Body Shops • Car Design • Automobile Equipment • Design Parking Garages and Lots	• Construction of Factories Specializing in Food • Modeling of Kitchens • Designing Restaurants	• Office of Tourism • Urban Tourism • Promotion of Historic Buildings • Monument Preservation • Publication of Tourist Guides	
2 **TOURISM**	• Financing Tourism Projects • Internal Auditor for Hotel	• Automobile Clubs (AAA,...) • Car Rental • Organize Driving Tours • Urban Parking • Exhibition Shows for Automobiles	• Import and Export of Exotic Products • Exotic Restaurants • Publishing of Restaurant Guides • Aviation Specializing in Tourism • Food Logistics		
3 **FOOD**	• Restaurant Entrepreneur • Purchasing for Hospital Cafeteria • Food Broker	• Meal Delivery to Homes • Catering Service			
4 **AUTOMOBILE**	• Automobile Leasing • Car Distribution • Sponsoring of Car Races • Automobile Insurance				
5 **FINANCE**					

Processing your discoveries (continued)

The ball is now in your court!

In the table on the next page, write in your five preferred fields of interest (from page 5.21). List them once in the heads of the columns (A, B, C,....) and once in the sides of the rows (1, 2, 3,....). Then fill out all the empty boxes at the crossroads of the columns and rows (A1, B2, C2,....). List two to six specific fields for each box. From these fields select the two or three fields which attract you most and circle them.

Processing your discoveries (continued)

Combining Your Fields of Interest

	A	B	C	D	E
1					
2					
3					
4					
5					

6

YOUR TARGET JOB: TITLE AND FIELD COMBINED

Congratulations! You now have all the building blocks needed to define your target job—the one that should bring you happiness and satisfaction.

Your Target Job: Title and Field Combined

You have now reached the final stage—the stage where all the pieces of your career puzzle come together. To make effective and productive choices, remember to always listen more to passion than to reason and not to be concerned if certain fields seem narrow.

To define your target job as narrowly as possible, you must identify one or both of the two key components of a job:

> ➤ the title which you want to hold; and

> ➤ the field in which you want to work.

A title is difficult and often useless to define before meeting and talking to some people who work in the field in which you are interested. If you define a title before meeting with people in your field of interest, it is often merely an academic and theoretical exercise.

In any case, the title does not help you determine names of organizations that you can approach. You will find those names by narrowing down your target job. To help you better understand, here is an illustration.

Example of the Creation of a Target Job

Here is an example of a job seeker who used this "job-creation" procedure to generate a table of target jobs. After you have examined it, proceed in the same way for your own situation.

Creation

In each of the three columns (A, B, C), the names of titles or responsibilities which interest the candidate are listed.

She has identified her talents (transferable skills) and wishes to have:

> ➤ some responsibilities in marketing;

> ➤ some general secretarial duties; and

> ➤ some responsibilities in data processing.

Creation (continued)

On each of the lines under "Field," nine specific fields are listed, which were defined by the candidate. She used the examples of overlapping fields of interest given earlier in this book (pages 5.02-5.04). Here are her preferred fields:

➤ Rental Cars

➤ Body Shops

➤ Road Signaling

➤ Air Traffic Controlling

➤ Interior Design of Airplanes

➤ Catering for Airlines

➤ Musical Therapy

➤ Cassette Sales to Airlines

➤ Philharmonic Orchestra

Verification

Each time a column (A, B, C) crosses a row (1-9), a target job is produced. Target jobs are the combination of a letter and number: A1, B5, C3, etc.

The candidate indicated her reaction to each target job on the chart. To evaluate each opportunity, she was given five possibilities to choose from:

➤ *Yes*   If the job really attracted her.

➤ *Maybe*   If the job was somewhat interesting to her.

➤ *No*   If she did not feel qualified for the job and had no interest in training for it.

➤ *No/Yes*   If she did not feel qualified for the job but was willing to acquire the necessary qualifications to attain it.

➤ *None*   If the target job was nonexistent.

Verification (continued)

FIELDS	TITLE A Marketing	TITLE B General Secretarial	TITLE C Data Processing
1 Rental cars	maybe	yes	no / yes
2 Body shops	yes*	maybe	maybe
3 Road signaling	no / yes	maybe	no / yes
4 Air traffic controlling	no	yes*	no / yes*
5 Interior design of airplanes	yes***	yes***	yes*
6 Catering for airlines	no	no / yes	maybe
7 Musical therapy	maybe	no / yes	maybe
8 Cassette sales to airlines	maybe	yes**	yes *
9 Philharmonic orchestra	no	yes **	yes*

Prioritization

Because she indicated "yes" to several of the target jobs, she then allocated stars to those boxes in order to prioritize them.

She allocated:

*** for target jobs which seemed ideal;

** for target jobs which really attracted her; and

* for target jobs which were okay.

Here are the candidate's final choices:

Rank	Title	Field
1 ***	Marketing	Interior design of airplanes
2 ***	General Secretarial	Interior design of airplanes
3 **	General Secretarial	Cassette sales to airlines
4 **	General Secretarial	Philharmonic Orchestra
5 *	Marketing	Body shops
6 *	General Secretarial	Air Traffic Controlling
7 *	Data Processing	Catering for airlines
8 *	Data Processing	Philharmonic Orchestra

Identifying Your Target Job

Creation

You can now proceed in the same way to define your target jobs by following the steps used in the preceding exercise.

In the table on the next page:

> ➤ at the top of each column, list titles which inspire you. Do not be too specific; and

> ➤ write on each of the 10 lines the narrowly defined fields which you identified in the exercise on page 5.25.

Creation (continued)

FIELDS	TITLE A	TITLE B	TITLE C
1			
2			
3			
4			
5			
6			
7			
8			
9			
10			

Verification

Now, fill in each of the empty boxes with one of the following choices:

➤ *Yes*   If the job really attracts you.

➤ *Maybe*   If the job is somewhat interesting to you.

➤ *No*   If you do not feel qualified for the job and have no interest in training for it.

➤ *No/Yes*   If you do not feel qualified for the job but are willing to acquire the necessary qualifications to attain it.

➤ *None*   If the target job is nonexistent.

Prioritization

Finally, allocate stars to prioritize your "yes" answers:

*** for target jobs that seem ideal;

** for target jobs that really attract you; and

* for target jobs that you like.

Compiling Your Discoveries

General Summary*

You can now summarize all the work that you have done by filling out the tables below.

I Would Like to Do the Following Jobs

RANK	TITLE	FIELD
1		
2		
3		

My Ideal People Environment

1. _____
2. _____
3. _____
4. _____
5. _____

With My Ideal Working Conditions

1. _____
2. _____
3. _____
4. _____
5. _____

*Inspired by Richard Nelson Bolles in his book, "What Color is your Parachute?" published by Ten Speed Press.

USING THE PIE METHOD IN THE JOB SEARCH

This very simple technique will help you land your ideal job.
Hurry and turn the page to begin…

The PIE Method

Origin, Principles, and Application of the PIE Method

Origin

You have probably practiced the PIE Method … without realizing it.

John Crystal is the "spiritual father" of the PIE Method.

During World War II, John Crystal was an active member of the American counterintelligence organization; some people might say he was a spy. He was an exceptional secret agent and carried out vital information missions through his ability to fluently speak foreign languages (French, Italian, German…), as well as his observational and analytical skills.

After the war, Crystal became a career counselor, assisting people who were changing jobs or careers. He taught—with great success—the information-gathering principles that he used to collect information during the war.

He stressed to his clients that gathering information is the first thing they need to do before approaching an organization and applying for a job. He strongly recommended investing time to gather information through "Information interviews." He taught that once a job seeker gathers the relevant information, it becomes easy to move toward "Employment interviews."

Meeting one day with a group of former diplomats searching for jobs, Crystal was stricken by their shyness. These people had met heads of states and VIP's throughout the world but did not feel comfortable conducting "Information interviews." He recommended that they try practicing interviews. To help them, he invented practice interviews or "Pleasure interviews," which consisted of meeting with people who have interests corresponding to one of your hobbies—in other words, meeting people just for fun to gather information about fields or subjects that are not job related.

Hence, the "practice field survey" was born. It emphasized both the key role of information in the job hunting process and the importance of not just one interview but three:

> ➤ the **P**leasure interview;
>
> ➤ the **I**nformation interview; and
>
> ➤ the **E**mployment interview.

These ideas are thoroughly explained with humor, heart, and talent by one of Crystal's closest friends, Richard N. Bolles, in the best-selling book, *What Color Is Your Parachute?*

It has also been applied successfully by tens of thousands of people in transition, both in America and Europe. It is structured to facilitate easy memorization and diminish the level of stress that accompanies every job hunt.

We have christened the approach: "The PIE Method."

> ➤ **P for Pleasure** (interviews for pleasure)
>
> ➤ **I for Information** (interviews for information)
>
> ➤ **E for Employment** (interviews for employment)

John Crystal was both intellectual and unassuming. He was a great humanist, a generous and cultured person who loved humor. He often used this illustration, "Never give a spy a weapon, he will be tempted to fight and become a soldier."

During information interviews, Crystal strongly insisted that the candidate avoid talking about employment (even if the other person introduces the subject).

Like the spy who would turn into a soldier, the candidate would be tempted to become a job seeker instead of an information gatherer if given the opportunity!

Principles

Career design and job hunting methods are often represented by icons or symbols. Professor Limoges, a famous Canadian professor in career design, uses the image of the "lucky clover." Three of the four lucky clover's leaves represent the past, the future, and the present.

The Past

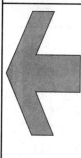

The past covers all of the things you have ever done … with pleasure. It is your assessment tool, a positive inventory of what you have achieved in the past.

It is especially concerned with:

➤ your talents (transferable skills);

➤ your preferred fields of interest;

➤ the characteristics of the people with whom you like to work; and

➤ your preferred working conditions.

The future focuses on everything you want to do which attracts you.

It is the target job that you envision.

It is your future job defined by:

➤ title (or function), and

➤ field (or industry).

The Future

The present covers whatever you are currently doing which coincides with what you have done with pleasure (past/assessment) and what you want to do (future/target).

It focuses on efficient job hunting techniques which you will use.

These techniques can be clustered into two groups. The first one consists of the techniques used to land an employment interview. The second group encompasses techniques used during the employment interview to convince the employer to hire you.

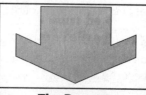

The Present

Principles (continued)

These three concepts can be represented by three circles.

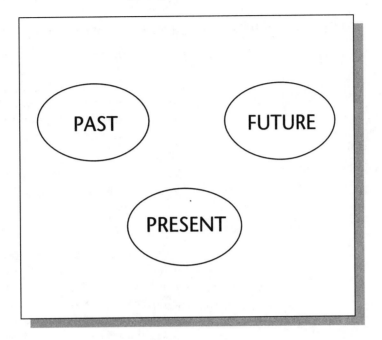

Being successful in your job search and managing your career later both depend on your ability to make these three circles overlap. Proceed in such a way that the target job you look for (future), corresponds as closely as possible with what you enjoy doing (past), while using the optimal job search techniques (present).

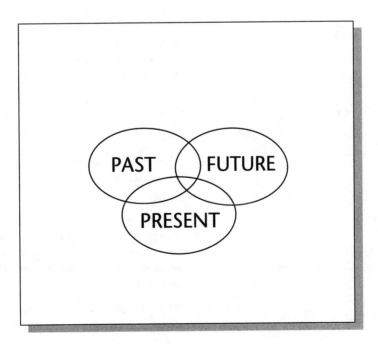

Principles (continued)

There are several mistakes job seekers make when matching the elements of past, present, and future.

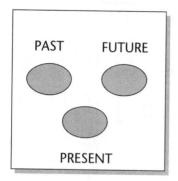

Mistake #1   **Failing to integrate the elements.**

Some people do an excellent job in terms of self-assessment (past), defining their target job (future), and using efficient job hunting techniques (present). However, they often do not combine the elements, frequently omitting the integration phase.

This process provides job seekers with the feeling of a job well done but does not propel them toward professional success.

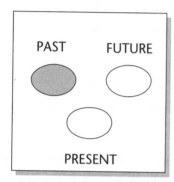

Mistake #2   **Limiting oneself to self-assessment only.**

Some concentrate on one aspect: self-assessment, self-assessment, self-assessment. This is especially typical with analytical and psychological approaches to job seeking. This method certainly reveals behavior patterns (past); however, nothing is done in terms of determining a target job (future) or conducting an efficient job search (present).

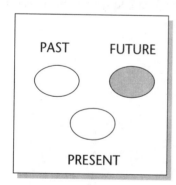

Mistake #3   **Concentrating solely on the target job.**

Some people define their target job (future) without considering any self-assessment (past). The criteria they use correspond weakly with their true aspirations. The techniques of job hunting (present) are neglected and not integrated into a consistent approach to finding a job.

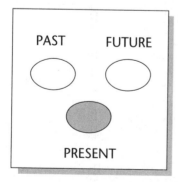

Mistake #4   **Concentrating solely on job hunting techniques.**

Some people concentrate only on job hunting techniques (present). Often, it is a case of a placement agency that wants to save time or cut corners by eliminating the phases of self-assessment (past) and target determination (future).

The job hunting process can be done very quickly; however, it can also be undone very quickly.

Principles (continued)

Mistake #5, 6, 7   Several other mistakes job seekers make include:

➤ Considering only self-assessment (past) and job hunting techniques (present);

➤ Concentrating on only self-assessment (past) and the target job (future); or

➤ Focusing on only job hunting techniques (present) and the target job (future).

The approach proposed in this book is simple and effective. Do not cheat yourself by skipping any of the three stages.

You could gain three days or three weeks bypassing one or more of these stages, but doing so may add considerable time to your job hunt. Even worse, you might accept an unsatisfying job that would keep you from doing what you really want to do for two to five years.

The PIE Method is designed to help you land your ideal job. These words might sound like an advertising slogan, but they mean exactly what they say. The method will work, but this requires that you work according to the method.

Don't cut corners. Don't skip exercises. Don't just "think it through" or try to imagine what a situation might be like. Do it! And if you don't like the results the first time, do it again.

This method has two marvelous advantages. First, everything is repeatable: you can do it again and again until you are satisfied with the results. Second, it can all be a lot more fun than you would have ever believed.

Application

You are able to use the PIE Method during several stages of your job search.

The PIE Method helps you according to the objectives you choose to pursue:

➤ before your job hunt during the orientation phase;

➤ at the beginning of or during your job search; and

➤ in many other instances.

■ Before your job hunt during the orientation phase

The PIE Method will help reveal more clearly:

➤ a field which you do not know well;

➤ a title which is new to you; or

➤ a job which is not familiar to you;

The PIE Method will help validate choices that you make concerning:

➤ field;

➤ title; or

➤ job.

The PIE Method will also help invalidate choices that you make, helping you avoid:

➤ a field which does not inspire you;

➤ a title for which you do not possess the needed skills; or

➤ a job which does not correspond to your aspirations.

The PIE Method can also give you the opportunity to arrange an internship in an organization which inspires and interests you.

■ At the beginning of or during your job search

The PIE Method can be useful in helping you find a job which matches your interests.

You can use it to get job interviews, in which you can negotiate different terms of employment:

➤ full-time;

➤ part-time; or

➤ temporary.

Application (continued)

■ On other occasions

In many other instances the PIE Method is excellent for:

- ➤ testing your preferred markets without any risk; and

- ➤ expressing to potential employers what skills and services you can offer them.

The PIE Method is systematically used by service organizations to:

- ➤ test the commercial feasibility of a project before launching it; and

- ➤ allow prospective clients to evaluate a "marvelous new service" before the service is actually introduced to the market.

The PIE Method: P Phase (Pleasure phase)

What is the objective of the Pleasure phase?

The main purpose of the P (Pleasure) phase is to allow you to familiarize yourself with the PIE Method, especially the interview process. This is a risk-free phase that really lets you "play" with the steps involved.

Once you discover the simplicity and efficiency of this method, you too will become a PIE Method enthusiast.

Once you have confidently adapted the PIE Method, you will naturally see how to use it during:

➤ The I (Information) phase, and

➤ The E (Employment) phase.

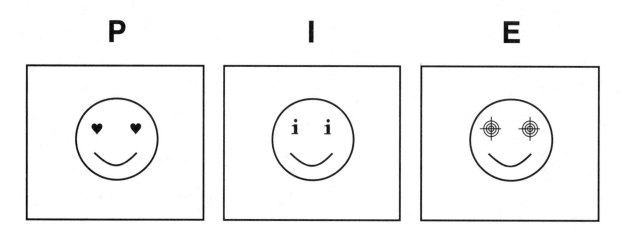

What topic should you choose?

To carry out your P (Pleasure) phase interviews, select a topic or subject that is not career-related:

> ➤ something that interests you;

> ➤ something that you have practiced or studied;

> ➤ something that puzzles you; or

> ➤ something that intrigues you.

The theme or subject could be:

> ➤ a hobby;

> ➤ a sport;

> ➤ a theme that interests you; or

> ➤ a cause that inspires you.

For example …

common topics:

- fashion
- computers
- antiques
- physical fitness

unusual topics:

- millionaires
- calligraphy
- UFOs
- llama farms

morbid topics:

- funeral homes
- cemetery keepers
- coroners
- morticians

artistic topics:

- photography exhibits
- art galleries
- jewelry makers
- sculptors

specific topics:

- homeless children
- sewage workers
- race car drivers
- street performers

With whom do you arrange interviews?

The people whom you choose to interview could be:

- Those who are actively engaged in a cause that inspires you;

- Those who share the same hobby as you and who are experts on the subject;

- Those who are very knowledgeable about something you admire and want to learn more about;

- Those who hold radical positions concerning issues which greatly interest you.

> **In short, the people you interview are those who possess experience in a subject which attracts you and from whom you can actually learn something.**

With whom should you conduct the Pleasure phase?

It is important to realize that during the phase of pleasure interviews, priority should be given to the people you meet and not to the organizations in which you meet them.

Your attention should be focused on the individual. These interviews often evolve with people in the same organization; however, we highly recommend interviewing people from several different organizations.

Do not go to see
an organization ...

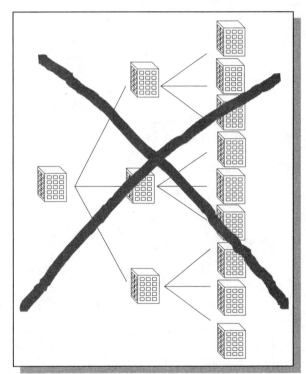

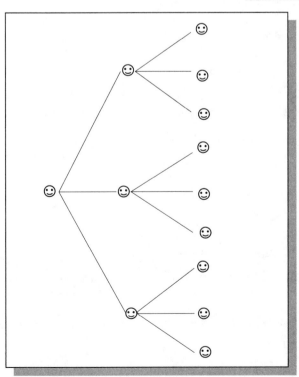

...but go to see specific people
within the organization.

Which geographical area should you choose?

When choosing a geographical area for conducting your P (Pleasure) phase interviews, select the most appropriate area—one where you would be able to carry out at least three interviews.

If the topic you choose is uncommon or highly specialized, you may need to travel to conduct your survey within your preferred geographical area.

This is an excellent reason for a one- or two-day trip in which you can combine research and pleasure.

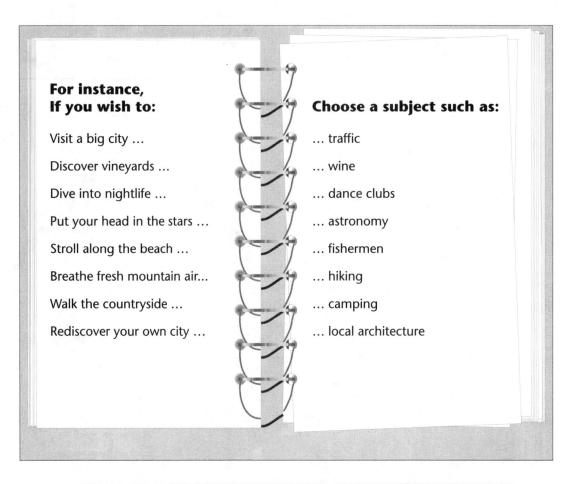

For instance,
If you wish to:

Visit a big city …

Discover vineyards …

Dive into nightlife …

Put your head in the stars …

Stroll along the beach …

Breathe fresh mountain air…

Walk the countryside …

Rediscover your own city …

Choose a subject such as:

… traffic

… wine

… dance clubs

… astronomy

… fishermen

… hiking

… camping

… local architecture

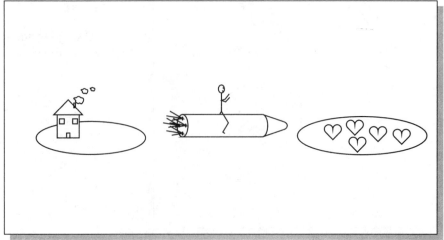

How do you get interviews?

Your approach during the P (Pleasure) phase of the PIE Method should be straightforward. Two approaches are possible.

Approach #1 The Cold Call

In the majority of cases dealing with subjects in which people are easily accessible, it is not necessary to make an appointment. Just go directly to the person, which is also known as "cold calling." On arrival, say that you would be grateful if he or she could answer a few quick questions.

Explain to the person that you realize his or her time is important, and offer to come back another day. Intrigued by curiosity and secure in the fact that the interview will be short, he or she will usually agree to talk to you right away.

If you encounter any type of resistance, do not insist. Simply tell the person the questions you want to ask, and offer to come back at a better time. The person will probably be impressed by your politeness and invite you to stay.

Approach #2 Phone Call

If you want to be more conservative in your approach, use the telephone.

Call if you are shy or fear rejection.

Call if the person you want to talk to is far away and you want to avoid an unnecessary trip.

Here are a few precautions to remember:

Do not disturb your interviewee; make an appointment with his or her assistant if it can be scheduled.

When you arrive for an interview; introduce yourself twice and spell your name clearly. Then briefly explain the purpose of your visit.

For each interview, prepare your text ahead of time and learn it by heart. When you request an interview, use the alternative technique of salespeople: offer the person two choices (either morning or afternoon, early in the week or later in the week).

How long do these interviews last?

During the P (Pleasure) phase, the length of interviews may vary widely. On average, plan on 10 to 20 minutes for an interview, especially if the person you are meeting is pressed for time. Often though, such interviews can last from 30 to 45 minutes.

Usually the interviews last between 15 and 30 minutes, but sometimes an interview can last twice as long or more. This is understandable because the subject you have chosen interests you and is usually one of your interviewee's passions. It is hardly surprising that interviews can last a long time when people talk about things they love.

As a general rule, the number one difficulty of the PIE Method is time management. Interviews often last much longer than expected. It will frequently be difficult for you to walk away from your interviewee once you have set that person "on fire." Be careful.

Remember, you are supposed to have fun. If it's not fun, assume that you're doing something wrong. Take a friend along and ask him or her to observe you. Afterwards, talk about how you did, asking specifically, "What could I have done better?" You'll be amazed at what you learn.

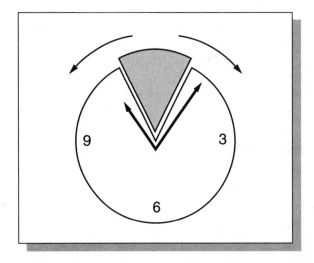

How many interviews should you conduct?

To learn the basic mechanics of the PIE Method, you should set up at least three interviews.

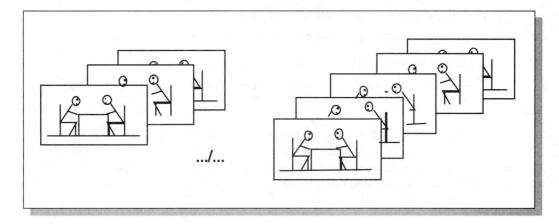

Determining the total number of pleasure interviews you want to conduct depends on how much you enjoy them and the extent to which you believe in the effectiveness of the PIE Method.

Intrigued by the interest they develop in their subject, the discoveries they make, and the contacts they establish, people frequently conduct from five to eight interviews during the P (Pleasure) phase.

You should go through as many interviews as it takes to convince you of the usefulness and efficiency of this method.

You have conducted a sufficient number of pleasure interviews when you have achieved the following three objectives.

Objective #1 Building a network.

You have mastered the technique necessary to build a network. You know how to obtain contact names, meet people you have never seen before, and turn them into points of support.

Objective #2 Getting people to talk.

You have acquired the art of getting your interviewees involved in a conversation that happens because you make it happen. These interviews are not random events like most conversations. You have a specific intention, and you proceed with a certain method. When you are comfortable with this, you are prepared for the next steps: phases I and E (interviews for Information and Employment).

Objective #3 Acquiring self-confidence.

You have developed sufficient confidence in yourself and in the PIE Method. You want to pursue the PIE Method and move on to the next phase: phase I (Information).

What questions should you ask?

During the P (Pleasure) phase of the PIE Method, you should ask four questions of each person you meet:

1. How did you get into this field/hobby/cause?

2. What do you like best about it?

3. What do you like least about it?

4. Could you give me the names and addresses of three other people who share the same interest?

The sequence in which these questions are asked usually ensures good results. We recommend that you follow this sequence because it has been proven through the experiences of hundreds of job seekers. Following is the sequence we propose you use for asking these questions, as well as objectives and reasons behind each question.

Question #1   "How did you get into this field/hobby/cause?"

Objective: To discover the 1001 avenues leading to the subject that you have chosen.

This first question calls for original and revealing answers from the interviewee. Its goal is to establish confidence and trust.

Who stumbled into the field/hobby/cause accidentally?

Who does not believe that the avenue he or she has followed in life is unique?

Which people do not like to talk about themselves?

Question #2   "What do you like best about it?"

Objective: To reveal everything which fascinates, excites, and stimulates people about the topic.

This second question calls for positive answers. It reinforces your interviewee's self-esteem and confidence. It puts him or her in a good mood for the next question. By gaining self-confidence, your interviewee will also gain confidence in you.

What questions should you ask? (continued)

Question #3 **"What do you like least about it?"**

Objective: To realize that even people who love a field/hobby/cause can identify some negative aspects of it.

This third question usually surprises the interviewee. The spontaneity of the person's answer will help you measure the level of trust you've been able to establish between you and the interviewee.

Question #4 **"Could you give me the names and addresses of other people who share the same interest?"**

Objective: To identify others who can help continue and complete your survey.

This fourth question may seem difficult for some of you.

However, you will be successful if you ask it at the end of the interview. At this stage, your relationship with the interviewee should be quite friendly. He or she will find it difficult to refuse to give you names of people who share the same enthusiasm about the topics you have discussed.

We have found that when people are enthusiastic about what they do, they want to share it. Therefore, they will tend to give you the names you need.

If you do not get the names you need, it is usually not your fault. You probably came across someone who does not like what he or she does for a living.

During the P (Pleasure) phase of the PIE Method, it is perfectly acceptable to include more questions if you wish. But first make sure to ask the four questions on these pages.

Should you take notes?

You do not need to take notes during the P (Pleasure) phase.

> ➤ If you call on them empty-handed …
> your contacts will not feel intimidated, which allows them to speak more freely.

The primary objective of the P phase is to pleasurably initiate you to the PIE Method. Pleasure is a word that often signifies the absence of constraints. If taking notes is a constraint for you, don't do it. The majority of people choose not to take notes during this phase.

However, always carry something with your name on it to give them—such as a business card—and a notebook for jotting down names, addresses, and directions.

> ➤ If you arrive at an interview and start unpacking writing material …
> you risk not bringing out spontaneous information that is usually only imparted in a relaxed, comfortable atmosphere.

Limit yourself to a notebook or a few blank sheets of paper to jot down what is said. If you feel the need, photocopy the questionnaire on the next page and take it with you.

Do not take a camera or camcorder except under special circumstances.

Should you take notes? (continued)

	P.I.E. QUESTIONNAIRE PHASE P

SUBJECT: _____

VISIT: 1. 2. 3. 4. 5. *(circle the corresponding number).*

PERSON INTERVIEWED: _____
_____

LOCATION: _____
_____

	QUESTIONS	ANSWERS
?	*How did you get involved in this field/hobby/cause?*	
+	*What do you like best about it?*	
—	*What do you like least about it?*	
	*Could you give me the names and addresses of three people who share the same interest?*	

How do you obtain names?

■ Asking for names

The strength of the PIE Method consists of building a network with the names you obtain from the people you meet.

The most difficult interview to get is the first one of each phase.

You do not always have a recommendation for the first interview.

But usually for the second interview you do have the advantage of someone's recommendation. Because you can mention the name of someone the person knows, you are not a stranger bothering that person. The red carpet unfolds, and the conditions for success are ideal.

When meeting the third interviewee, you can mention the name of the person whom you just met and who recommended him or her as a contact. Because all of your contacts work in the same field, you can drop the names of everyone you have met. This technique reinforces your image and unties tongues.

How do you obtain names? (continued)

■ **Whom should you choose as the first person to interview?**

Always choose somebody who does not intimidate you and whom you admire and respect. This person can be:

➤ A friend

➤ A relative

➤ Somebody you talked to on the telephone

➤ A friend of a friend

How do you obtain names? (continued)

■ Why should you ask for several names?

It is highly recommended that at the end of each interview, you ask for several names to help multiply the wonderful effects of the PIE Method! Each person that you meet mentions at least three names. Each of these three people, in turn, mentions three other names, and so on. The list of names you obtain often becomes quite impressive.

Because things never go as well as hoped, some people who are recommended to you will be inaccessible or unfeasible.

Therefore, it is always wise to have more names than you think you need.

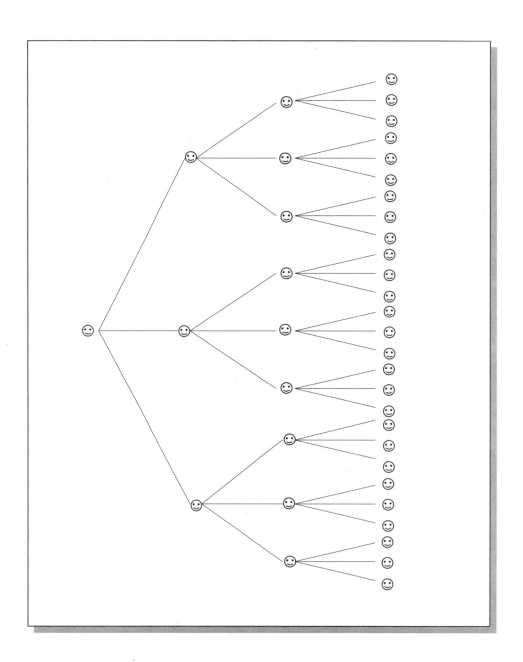

How do you obtain names? (continued)

■ Whom should you interview?

If you obtain three names during an interview, you should not limit yourself by meeting with each of those three people.

Your survey will be more interesting and thorough if you meet one of these people, then a second person mentioned by the first one, then a third one mentioned by the second and so on …

This method of proceeding will make your survey more diversified and effective. You will reap the benefits of this approach during the next step of the PIE Method—the I (Information) phase.

Approach #1   Exploring your network laterally for four interviews.

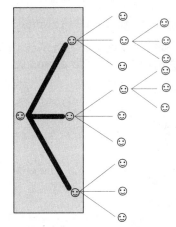

Approach #2   Exploring your network vertically for four interviews.

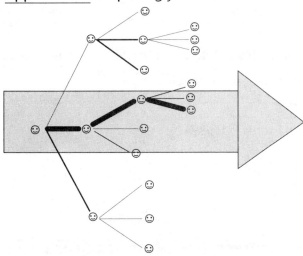

How do you obtain names? (continued)

■ How do you phrase your question to get names?

Tell your interviewee that you are excited about what you have learned and that you would like to know more about the subject.

Ask if he or she could give you two or three names of other people who share the interest you want to investigate.

As soon as names are mentioned, jot them down and ask for their addresses. Then use the "escalation" process by asking the three following questions. Observe the following sequence carefully and pause between each question.

➤ May I call on these people?

➤ May I mention your name?

➤ May I say that you recommended I call on them?

As soon as you receive a positive answer to one question move on to the next one.

The fact that you are proceeding through careful steps will show your interviewee that you are respectful and discreet. Because these qualities are often hard to find, this person will probably support you. You will have acquired an ally.

How do you obtain names? (continued)

■ **Ask for names of people, not names of organizations!**

If you are given names of organizations or a list of companies instead of people's names, you might say:

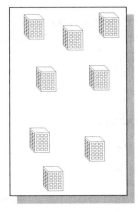

"Thank you very much for this list. In your opinion, what are the three to five organizations I should approach first?"

Then, once you have been given the names of three to five organizations, say:

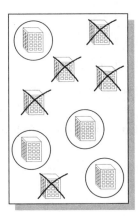

"Would you please give me one person's name to contact in each of these organizations?"

How do you build a network?

In the PIE Method, the first step—the first interview—is the one that requires the most effort from you.

If this first interview goes well, you will get three names to help you begin building your network. Each of these three names should get you another three names, soon you will have nine names, and so on …

This technique might remind you of the famous tale of "the seeds of wheat."

Once upon a time, a king wanted to thank a man who had rendered him a wonderful service. The king asked the man what he wanted most on earth. The man took a chess board and asked to be given …

1   seed of wheat for the first square,

2   seeds of wheat for the second square,

4   seeds of wheat for the third square,

8   seeds of wheat for the fourth square,

16   seeds of wheat …

The king was delighted with the modesty of the wish and granted it immediately. He was shocked when he realized that all of the wheat in his kingdom or even the whole world was not enough to fill the chess board!

The same goes for the network you construct with the PIE Method.

➤ At the first level: the first person whom you meet mentions three names.

➤ At the second level: each of these three people provides you with three other names, which gives you a total of nine names.

➤ At the third level: on the average each of these nine people provides you with three names, which leads you to 27 names.

➤ At the fourth level: each of these 27 people provides you with three names, which results in 81 names!

…soon you will be drowning in names.

How do you build a network? (continued)

As you conduct your survey, you will find that some people whose names have been given to you have no time to meet with you, others are sick, some are out of town, etc.

This type of situation can easily affect two out of three people. Therefore, have vision!

Whenever you meet someone, do not limit yourself to getting only one name; make sure to get at least three to five names.

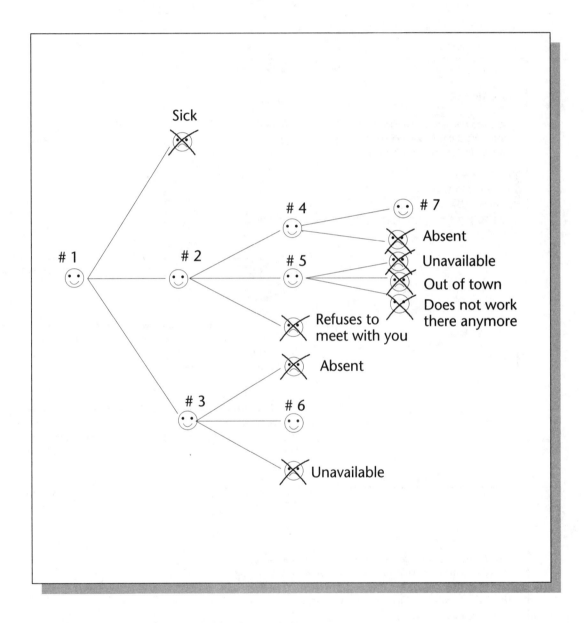

How do you say thank you?

On the same day of your visit or soon after, write a thank-you note to each of the people you met. Use a simple thank-you card.

Sign your name clearly so that the recipient will be able to recognize you and include your address if you wish.

Here are a few examples that we selected. They were successfully used by people who have practiced this method.

Anytown, June 12, 19XX

Dear Ms. Hall,

I want to thank you wholeheartedly for the very warm welcome that you extended during my visit.
I was delighted with the interview.

Alice Bertram
109 East Elm Street
Anytown, USA

Anytown, May 8, 19XX

Dear Mr. Noble,

A thousand thanks for the twenty minutes we spent together today. I was excited by the visit and learned a lot in a short amount of time.
Hope to see you again.

Debbie Warren
315 Harbor Pointe Drive
Anytown, USA

Anytown, August 13, 19XX

Dear Mr. Pitt,

I would like to express sincerely my pleasure with the visit we shared yesterday morning. Your career as an actor is extremely exciting.
Thank you for taking the time to meet with me.

Deborah Jones
1511 Success Drive
Anytown, USA

How do you say thank you? (continued)

Anytown, March 26, 19XX

Dear Ms. Blaine,

The interview that we held recently was informative and helpful.
The information you provided has helped me toward making my decision.
Thank you for your assistance.

Kathleen Kennedy
3486 Arbor Lane
Anytown, USA

Anytown, July 20, 19XX

Dear Mr. Bright,

I sincerely thank you for the time you shared with me to answer my questions Tuesday afternoon. Your photography hobby is quite exciting.
Your generosity is much appreciated.

Diane Guy
9635 North Highgate Circle
Anytown, USA

Anytown, August 30, 19XX

Dear Mrs. Andrews,

I was quite impressed by the information that you provided during our interview on Monday morning.
I want to thank you for your very warm welcome.

Patricia Peaker
101 North Linwood Avenue
Anytown, USA

Anytown, February 17, 19XX

Dear Miss Carfrey,

Many thanks to you for revealing the secrets of your work to me.
I will soon be getting in touch with the people you mentioned to me, and I will keep you informed of my progress.

Jason Hall
111 South Rogers Street
Anytown, USA

How do you say thank you? (continued)

Anytown, September 7, 19XX

Dear Mr. Boggess,

This thank-you note is to express my deep appreciation for answering my questions about fund-raising yesterday morning. Thanks to you, I now have a much clearer vision of your field.

Gloria Griffin
230 Belvedere Drive
Anytown, USA

Anytown, December 11, 19XX

Dear Mrs. Smith,

I want to thank you for taking time out of your busy schedule to meet with me and providing me with names of other people I can contact.
I was very impressed with your knowledge and dedication.

Robert Scott
1807 Hoyt Avenue
Anytown, USA

Anytown, August 4, 19XX,

Dear Mr. Wallace,

I want to thank you for spending 20 minutes of your time to answer my questions this afternoon about historic churches in Anytown.
Your enthusiasm is contagious.

Donna Forey
153 Gaines Street
Anytown, USA

Anytown, September 6, 19XX,

Dear Miss Williams,

Many thanks for your warm welcome. All of the information that you provided me will be very useful.

Emily Jacobs
838 Crooked Lane
Anytown, USA

What is the length of the Pleasure phase?

The P (Pleasure) phase of the PIE Method can be completed in a short amount of time, usually in a day or two.

Because you choose the field you want to investigate, you can select one which is easily accessible to you.

Experience shows that it is possible to conduct an average of three interviews in half a day, (this comes from a survey of 249 people who carried out between three and four interviews in one afternoon).

In the most difficult circumstances, this phase should last a week at the most.

In most cases, you do not arrange interviews ahead of time.

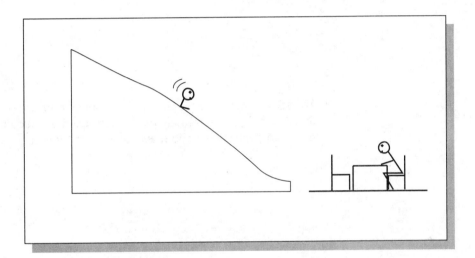

You can, however, arrange the interviews by telephone the day before or even the same day.

What are the dangers of the Pleasure phase?

The P (Pleasure) phase of the PIE Method presents no danger whatsoever.

The field that you select for your survey should not be linked in any way to the field in which you want to work.

There are, however, two difficulties which you may encounter.

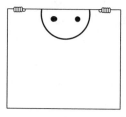

- The first difficulty is trouble contacting people who share the interest you have chosen because those people may be very busy or always on the road.

    For example: detectives, journalists, politicians, celebrities, etc.

- The second difficulty is leaving the people whom you interview. Some people are extremely passionate about the subject you are discussing with them and may not want to let you go!

The PIE Method: I Phase (Information phase)

What are the objectives of the Information phase?

The objectives of the I (Information) phase are:

➤ to teach you about jobs which you envision having;

➤ to validate a thorough investigation into a particular job;

➤ to help you make choices; and

➤ to give you arguments to be more convinced and convincing during your job search (phase E).

What fields do you choose?

The fields that you choose for interviews during the I (Information) phase are those corresponding to your ideal target jobs.

For example:
If you wish to become …

- an environmental lawyer for an organization that works for the protection of nature

- a surgeon in the Army

- a trilingual secretary in an industry which imports and exports food products

Find and meet

… lawyers who work, preferably, for organizations concerned with the protection of nature

… military surgeons

… secretaries, trilingual if possible, in a business which imports and exports food products

Your information phase must therefore be conducted with people who work in the job you envision doing.

 Be careful …

Ideally your interviews should not be held with people who can help you find work in this industry. They definitely must not take place with a person who could become your boss! These interviews must also not be conducted with the bosses of those who do the job you wish to do!

> **Your information phase survey must be centered on the people who do the jobs you want to do (your future colleagues)… and not on those who have the power to hire you.**
>
> **This is the basic rule of the PIE Method! It is also the one broken most often!**

What fields do you choose? (continued)

You may hesitate to do your information phase survey in the geographical area where you want to become established. The area is sometimes too narrow, or the organizations within it are not numerous enough.

In this case, only one solution exists: move the survey! Do your I (Information) phase in another geographical area—maybe another city or town in your state.

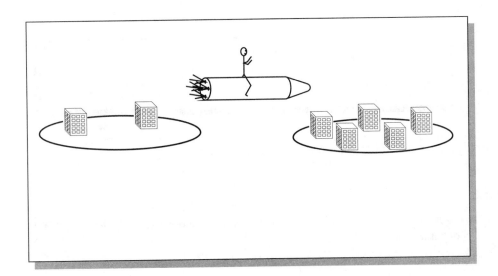

With whom do you arrange interviews?

The people whom you speak to in the information phase should be potential colleagues.

> **You must meet**
>
> **People who work in the job or field which attracts you.**

This cannot and must not lend itself to ambiguity.

Remember! Be clever and precise when asking questions during information phase interviews.

> **Only interview**
>
> **Future colleagues**

It would be a major mistake to interview three types of people.

 Avoid:

➤ your future supervisor, the person in charge, the president or director of the organization;

➤ the public relations manager; and

➤ the director of human resources.

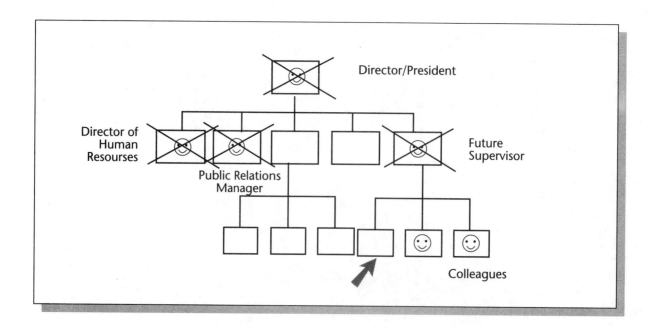

With whom do you arrange interviews? (continued)

 Avoid your potential supervisor (or the person in charge of the organization).

Do not interview, under any circumstances, a person who holds a position above the one which interests you or a person in charge of the organization which attracts you. Instead of providing you with information, the person will ask you to provide information about yourself! But, having not completed the information phase, you still don't know what should be said... about you!

 Avoid the public relations manager.

Avoid being met by the head of public or external relations for the organization which attracts you. This person's job is definitely to provide information pertaining to the organization, but you are researching the positions your future colleagues hold. At the end of a visit with a public relations manager, you will be familiar with the walls, the corridors, the flow charts, and the products of the organization but... very little about the title which attracts you.

 Avoid the director of human resources.

Don't make a mistake here either! You are gathering information and not yet looking for a job. Your objective is to have someone who does the job which attracts you explain its title, not a third party.

With whom do you arrange interviews? (continued)

If people doing the job you want to investigate do not exist in your geographical area, two solutions are available.

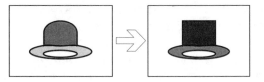

Solution #1 Identify a substitute job.

Identify a job similar to the one which attracts you. Then, conduct your information phase interviews with people who hold this job in your geographical area.

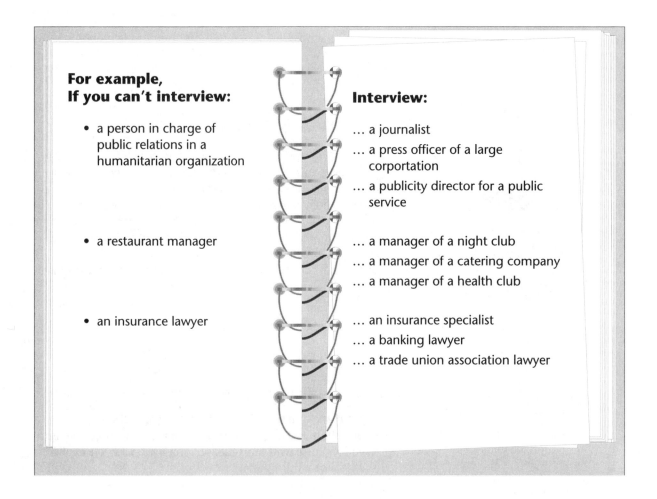

**For example,
If you can't interview:**

- a person in charge of public relations in a humanitarian organization

- a restaurant manager

- an insurance lawyer

Interview:

… a journalist

… a press officer of a large corportation

… a publicity director for a public service

… a manager of a night club

… a manager of a catering company

… a manager of a health club

… an insurance specialist

… a banking lawyer

… a trade union association lawyer

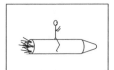

Solution #2 Go outside your geographical area

Interview outside your geographical area people who do the job that attracts you.

With which organizations do you conduct the Information phase?

Two different viewpoints concerning the choice of organizations exist for the I (Information) phase survey of the PIE Method.

It is up to you to adopt the strategy that suits you best.

Strategy #1 The proximity strategy

Choose organizations in which you wish to work and have at least one person doing the job which interests you.

Go there with the sole purpose of gathering information.

Once there, meet with the person who does the job which attracts you. Remember! Do not interview this person's boss.

Occasionally, the person whom you meet may be in need of an associate or temporary assistant.

Be careful! Do not bring up, in any way, the possibility of temporary or permanent employment by the organization! You are there solely to acquire information and not to get a job.

Strategy #2 The cautious strategy

Choose organizations that are located in your preferred geographical area but are ones in which you would certainly not want to work.

If this is not possible, go outside the geographical area where you envision working and select organizations in a large city close to that zone.

Which geographical area should you choose?

If the geographical area in which you wish to work is economically developed and offers a concentration of organizations, don't hesitate to choose it as a region for research and investigation.

If, however, the geographical area in which you would like to work is small and lacks opportunity, choose a different region for your research during the I (Information) phase. For example, select a large city close to your home. Arrange to hold your interviews in a one- or two-day span. This may be difficult to coordinate at first, but it will quickly become child's play.

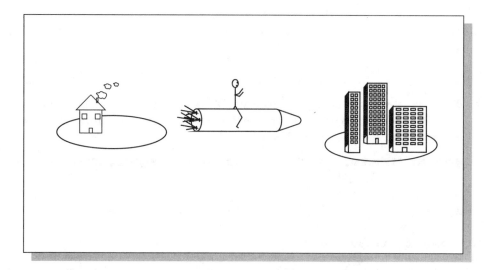

How do you set appointments?

Three formulas are possible for setting appointments. Choose the one that suits you and best corresponds with the type of person you want to interview.

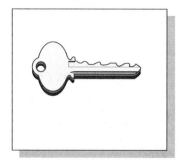

Formula #1 The "Knock on the Door"

Present yourself without previous contact. You will have—(70 percent of the people who use this formula do)—legs like jelly and sweaty palms!

Formula #2 The Telephone Call

By telephone, arrange a suitable date for an appointment. Speak to the assistant or secretary of the person you wish to meet.

Avoid speaking on the telephone to the person you wish to meet. You risk conducting your interview over the phone!

Formula #3 The Letter

Send a letter asking for an interview and which clearly explains the reasons for your request.

Don't forget to mention the name of the person who gave you the address, and by whom you have been recommended. Take the initiative to telephone after sending your letter (see #2 above).

How long do these interviews last?

The ideal length of an interview in the information phase is one which does not intrude on the other person's time!

Rather than think of length, think of an "hour" in the day or a "day" in the week. First determine which hour or day will least upset your interviewer's schedule. Then arrange a suitable length of time. If the person whom you will meet has an assistant or a secretary, he or she should be able to tell you the best time to arrange an interview.

Next, avoid being vague regarding the length of the interview.

Don't use terms like "a few minutes," "10 or 20 minutes," or "a brief amount of time."

Propose either 10, 15, or 30 minutes.

A good idea is to propose a length of time and "justify it" by the hour chosen for the appointment. For example, if the employees leave work at 6 p.m., say:

"Would you be able to meet for 10 minutes at 5:50?"

Interviews often extend beyond the time initially planned. If this happens, this is what you can do. When the predetermined time for the end of your interview arrives, glance at your watch and say that you do not want to take advantage of his or her time.

If the person wishes to continue the discussion, ask how much time he or she can allow, and don't forget to thank them for this extra time.

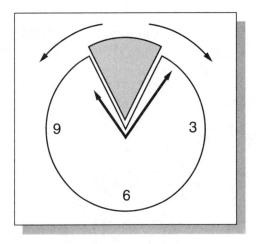

How many interviews should you have?

■ Minimum number of interviews

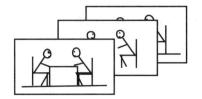

The minimum number of interviews necessary to evaluate a function is three.

■ Optimum number of interviews

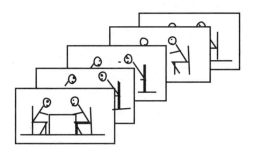

It is smarter to conduct four or five interviews. The greater the number of interviews you conduct, the greater your chances will be of realizing one or more of the following three discoveries.

Discovery #1 Your "Adoptive Godparent"

By multiplying your number of interviews, you might have the chance to meet the person who has had a professional history similar to yours or the one that awaits you. This person will be sympathetic toward you. He or she will have lived through the experiences awaiting you and may help you elude the traps and difficulties lying ahead.

This person—your adoptive godparent—will probably render you a double service:

➤ This person will treat you sympathetically because in a way you resemble him or her. He or she will relive through you, and thanks to you, a career turning point in which he or she negotiated and succeeded. This person will probably be delighted to support and advise you.

➤ He or she will indicate the names of people in the same title who have had this particular type of professional history. Familiar with all kinds of people in the profession, he or she will be pleased to integrate you.

Have you ever noticed your ability to spot the people who drive the same car as you, wear the same clothes, or have a characteristic similar to your own?

How many interviews should you have? (continued)

■ Optimum number of interviews

Discovery #2 The Hidden Problems

By multiplying your number of interviews, you may be able to reveal the inconveniences, hidden problems, or "the skeletons in the closet" of the job you envision … they exist in every profession.

Discovery #3 Your "Cup of Tea"

By conducting multiple interviews, you may discover that several methods for doing the same title exist. You will also note that there are many different ways to find satisfaction in the same job.

You will then be able to direct yourself toward the right method for accomplishing the job which attracts you. You can focus on doing what our British cousins call your "cup of tea!"

How many interviews should you have? (continued)

■ Optimum number of interviews

In the course of the information phase, you will note:

➤ certain tasks are frequently cited—these constitute the heart of the job which you envision;

➤ other tasks are mentioned much more rarely—these are very different or even unexpected tasks.

This diversity allows you to clarify your views on the way that you wish to do the job which attracts you.

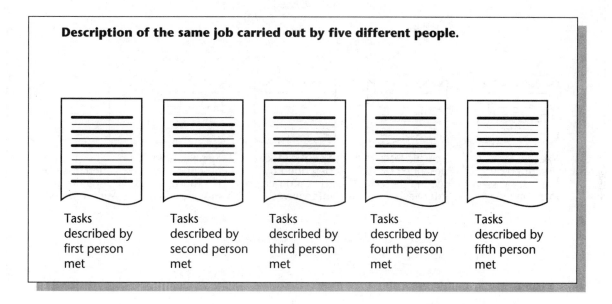

Description of the same job carried out by five different people.

Tasks described by first person met

Tasks described by second person met

Tasks described by third person met

Tasks described by fourth person met

Tasks described by fifth person met

How many interviews should you have? (continued)

■ Optimum number of interviews

Gross results

Each of these five cards describes the same job viewed by five different people. Each job is perceived and described differently by five people whom you interviewed.

Certain tasks are commonly described. These are shown by a thick line.

Other tasks vary from one description of the job to another. These are shown by a thin line.

Common tasks
described by the
five people
interviewed
(heart of the job)

Specific tasks
described by
the first person
interviewed

Specific tasks
described by the
second person
interviewed

Specific tasks
described by
the third person
interviewed

Specific tasks
described by
the fourth person
interviewed

Specific tasks
described by
the fifth person
interviewed

Results after analyzing your survey

After a brief analysis, you will readily discern common tasks systematically cited by those people whom you interviewed. These tasks constitute the core of the job which you envision.

> **Therefore, no matter which organization you choose, you will be practically certain of having to assume the tasks pertaining to the core.**

In the E (Employment) phase, it will remain for you to simply prove that you are able to do these tasks.

How many interviews should you have? (continued)

■ **Optimum number of interviews**

Refine your actions

The more numerous your interviews are in the information phase, the better your ability will be to identify the strong points which you must include in the next phase: phase E (Employment). This is the phase in which you are going to negotiate your future employment.

These strong points are competencies you possess but may not always consider valuable. Frequently, they have become familiar and natural to you. They may seem banal to you, but—to your surprise—are much desired in the job for which you are aiming. You will rediscover through the PIE Method, values, competencies, and talents you possess and would not think of disclosing.

A bone surgeon specialist was asked, "How can you do what you do and like it?" After a long moment of reflection, he answered, "I like what I do. My greatest pleasure, beyond rendering a service, is to refine my actions!"

Each of us, if we like our job, experiences a certain pleasure in "refining our actions."

For example:

> ➤ an accountant likes to compile more quickly and accurately;

> ➤ a writer likes to write more concisely;

> ➤ a dentist likes to treat more gently;

> ➤ a seller likes to persuade more thoroughly; and

> ➤ a receptionist likes to listen more attentively.

How many interviews should you have? (continued)

■ Optimum number of interviews

What do you do if you don't have all the skills required to perform a particular job?

You are also able, thanks to the PIE Method, to identify your weaknesses and deficiencies for any job which you envision. The interviews you conduct enable you to learn how to precisely identify your weak points as well as your strong ones. The more interviews, the better.

Once your strengths and weaknesses are defined, you will be able to adopt one of the three following strategies.

Strategy #1 The "Ad-hoc" Job

Direct yourself toward organizations in which the job is carried out in such a way that your weaknesses and deficiencies do not constitute a major handicap or a risk of failure.

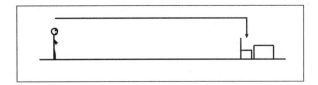

Strategy #2 The "Stop-gap" Job

You take a "stop-gap" job to acquire the things you lack or to consolidate those which you possess. This will allow you, afterwards, to target your ideal job.

The normal time people remain in a "stop-gap" job is from 6 to 24 months. It can be held in the same organization as your ideal job or another one.

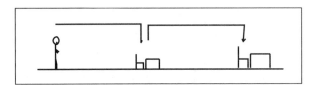

Strategy #3 The Training

You choose to pursue training that gives you the knowledge and skills you lack to do the job which inspires you.

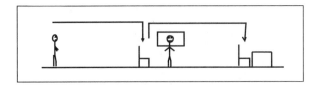

How many interviews should you have? (continued)

■ Optimum number of interviews

You can acquire this information through two different methods.

1. On a full-time basis, in a continuous and intensive way

A less-intensive approach will take you a few days or a few weeks. A more-intensive approach will continue over several months or up to one or two years.

Here are two examples:

A leisurely approach:

➤ three days exploring industrial marketing; or

➤ two to five days studying financial investing.

An intensive approach:

➤ three months exploring management control; or

➤ one year studying general management techniques.

2. On a part-time basis, in a less intensive way, spread over time

A relaxed approach will take a few evenings each week for one to three months. A more-intensive approach will cover several evenings each week for one to three years.

Here are two examples:

A leisurely part-time approach:

➤ four Saturdays exploring software data processing; or

➤ five evenings studying communication techniques.

An intensive part-time approach:

➤ two evenings per week for a year exploring human resources; or

➤ two days each month studying exportation.

How many interviews should you have? (continued)

■ **Optimum number of interviews**

Strategy #4 The "Replacement" Job

The job which you dream about may be impossible for you to obtain: schooling is too long, requires innate skills, etc.

Then identify a suitable replacement job.

Approach two or three people doing the job of which you dream and explain your limits and constraints to them. Ask them what they would choose as an alternative job or occupation if their job were to suddenly disappear.

Here are a few responses collected using this approach.

Thus, for example a ...   said his or her replacement job would be...

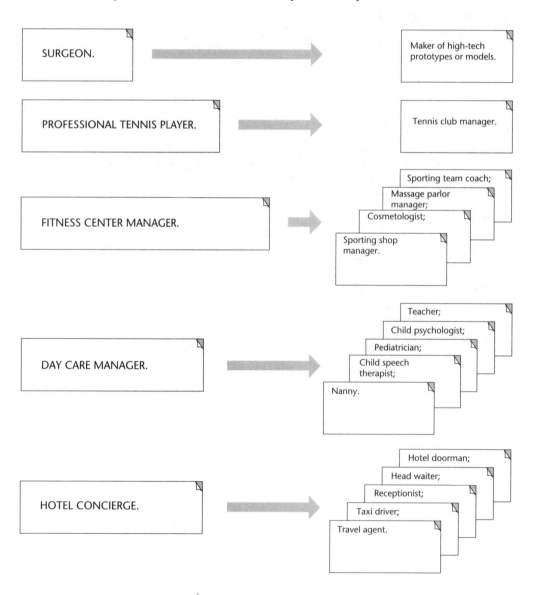

How many interviews should you have? (continued)

■ Probable number of interviews

The I (Information) phase of the PIE Method consists of collecting information that corresponds to the ideal job or title which you dream of holding.

To realize this survey, you must conduct three to five interviews for each job target envisioned.

Thus, if you envision three job targets, you must carry out three information phases; one I (Information) phase for each job target.

If you envision three job targets and a plan B job, you must conduct 12-20 interviews, (12 interviews = 4 jobs with 3 interviews for each target; 20 interviews = 4 jobs with 5 interviews for each target).

A plan B job is one you can fall back on if the moves you make toward your preferred jobs do not succeed. This is a contingency type job!

To simplify things, here is a diagram which summarizes the number of interviews you expect to conduct in the information phase.

Phase I Interviews	Number of interviews to conduct for each job target				
	Target job 1	Target job 2	Target job 3	Target job 4	**Total # of interviews**
Minimum # of interviews to conduct	3	3	3	3	12
Maximum # of interviews needed to reveal the complexity of the job target which you envision	5	5	5	5	20
# of interviews you expect to conduct	6	5	3	4	18
# of interviews you have effectively conducted					

What questions should you ask?

During the I (Information) phase of the PIE Method, ask six questions of each person you meet.

Each of the six questions targets a definite purpose. The order in which they are asked, therefore, has a strategic significance.

Question #1 How did you get to this position?

You will discover the 1001 ways which can lead to the position you envision.

This question pleases your interviewee because:

- it proves that you are interested in him or her;
- each person thinks his or her track record is unique;
- and people like to talk about themselves.

Question #2 What do you like most about this position?

You will verify if the job interests and excites you.

This question calls for various responses destined to reinforce the positive feeling developed from the person's answer to the first question.

Your interviewee gains confidence in himself or herself and also in you.

Question #3 What do you like least about this position?

You assure yourself that you are will be able to cope with the inherent difficulties of this type of position.

Because the interviewee has placed you in confidence by answering your first two questions, nothing will be held back, and you will benefit from this information. The "real truth" emerges.

What questions should you ask? (continued)

Question #4 What are the standard required tasks of this position?

All of the tasks that this type of position requires are enumerated and defined.

After having described much of the sensitive, subjective, and confidential aspects of the job, your interviewee is ready to impart first-hand information to you.

The tasks are probably given to you abundantly with great detail. Take advantage of this information to summarize a list of essential and secondary tasks.

Question #5 What skills are needed to complete these tasks successfully?

Make a list of the talents, competencies, knowledge, and personality traits necessary to carry out these tasks successfully. For each task, define the specific skills, transferable skills, and personality traits needed. This information will be very useful later.

Question #6 Could you please give me the names and addresses of three people who have the same job?

You obtain other names for following up and completing your survey.

This question is the finishing touch. It ends the interview. At the same time, it begins upcoming interviews by connecting you to the people you will meet.

Should you take notes?

A lot of information is going to be revealed to you during the course of your I (Information) phase interviews. If your memory is not your best ally, it would be unfortunate to allow such important information to be lost. Take notes!

During the I (Information) phase, it is sensible to take notes. Use either a notepad or a photocopy of the questionnaire on the following page.

When you take notes, be careful to:

> ➤ ask your interviewee in advance if it poses a problem;

> ➤ write in a nonsecretive way by leaving your notepad open on the desk;

> ➤ write fast to avoid interrupting the speech flow of your interviewee; and

> ➤ stop writing if the interview takes a confidential turn. In this case, put the notepad down and place your pen in a conspicuous manner on the desk.

> ➤ Look directly at your interviewee and through eye contact let him or her know: "I realize that what is going to be said is confidential."

Should you take notes? (continued)

P.I.E. QUESTIONNAIRE
PHASE I

SUBJECT: _____

VISIT: 1. 2. 3. 4. 5. *(circle the corresponding number).*

PERSON INTERVIEWED: _____

        LOCATION: _____

	QUESTIONS	ANSWERS
?	How did you get to this position?	
+	What do you like most about this position?	
—	What do you like least about this position?	
☁	What are the standard required tasks of this position?	
★	What skills are needed to complete these tasks successfully?	
⌒	Could you give me the names and addresses of three people who have the same job?	

How do you obtain names?

To obtain names to build your network, two formulas are possible.

Formula #1 Friends, third parties, and relatives

Here are the paths used most frequently with success to obtain names:

- a friend who knows someone who does the job which interests you;
- a friend or relative who does the job which interests you;
- a parent;
- a colleague;
- someone who knows someone;
- etc.

Formula #2 The telephone book and telephone

Sometimes you have no direct or indirect way of contacting someone in an organization. In this case, look in the telephone book to locate an organization that employs someone doing the job which interests you.

Then, call the organization.

Verify that the job exists in the organization and ask for the name(s) of the corresponding employee(s).

Then, it only remains for you to:

- write the person (if you are shy);
- telephone the person (if you are less shy or don't like writing); or
- go meet the person (having previously written or telephoned).

How do you obtain names? (continued)

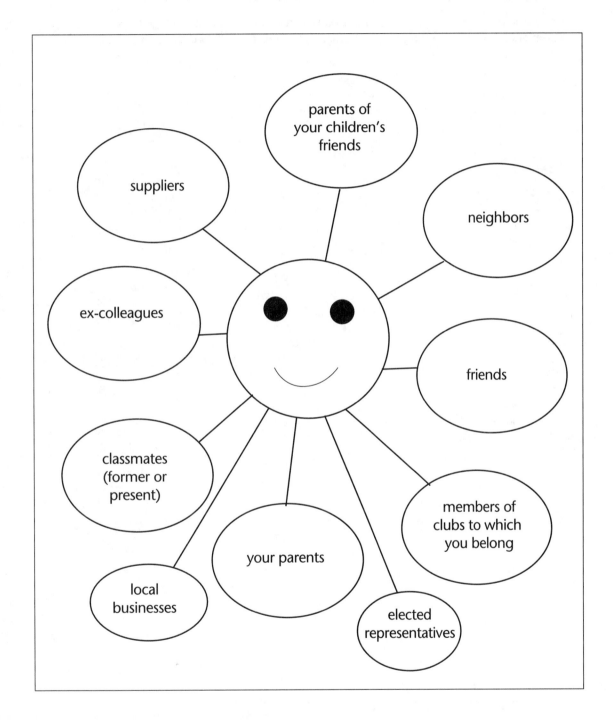

How do you build a network?

The principal method behind building a network in the information phase of the PIE Method is exactly the same as the one described for the preceding P (Pleasure) phase.

The same rules apply. The P (Pleasure) phase allows you to practice without risk! Repeat the experience by applying the same principles as before. You will find the same success.

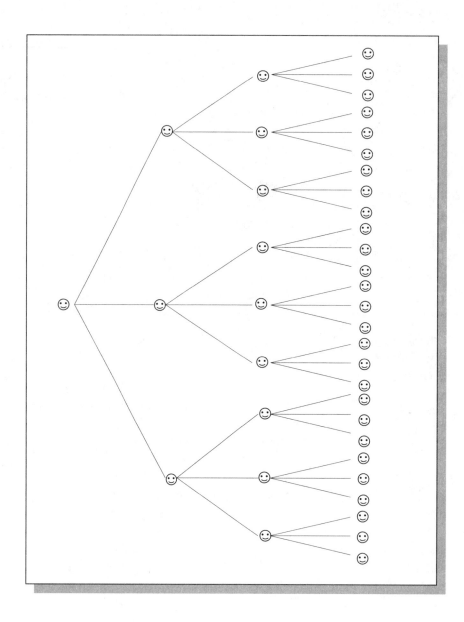

How do you say thank you?

On the day of your visit or soon thereafter, send a thank-you note to the person who took the time to meet with you.

A simple card or note, handwritten or typed, is acceptable.

> **Do not forget to include your accurate name and address, in case the person wishes to contact you again!**

Here are some thank-you cards sent by job seekers who were happy with the information interviews they obtained.

Anytown, June 25, 19XX

Mr. Brown,

I would like to extend my gratitude for your warm reception and the information which you gave me.
My visit with you was very beneficial to my search.
Thanks again.

Victoria Andersen
17 Ring Place
Anytown

Anytown, July 2, 19XX

Miss Hill,

Thank you very much for the interview on July 1 in your office at The Olympia Hotel.
Your knowledge about the tourism industry and specifically hotel management will be a great help in my final career decision.

Paul Webster
23 Grouse Avenue
Anytown

Anytown, April 24, 19XX

Mrs. Pollard,

A million thanks for all of the information you imparted to me concerning your career.
I will definitely heed your advice and research writing opportunities with local newpapers and publishers.
Hope to see you again soon.

Frank Newberry
435 St. John Street
Anytown

How do you say thank you? (continued)

Anytown, August 13, 19XX

Mr. Prescott,
Thank you so much for answering my questions this morning.
Your responses were informative and insightful.
I now have a much better idea of what your position as public
relations director entails. I find your job exciting and fulfilling
and hope to follow in your footsteps.

Heather Brooks
234 New Jersey Avenue
Anytown

Anytown, December 12, 19XX

Miss Kaplan,

I want to thank you for allowing me to interview yesterday.
I was delighted with our discussion. It has helped me to better
define my career objectives in the biology field.

Randy White
817 North Washington
Anytown

Anytown, January 14, 19XX

Mr. Ervin,

Thank you for the hospitality you extended to me during our
recent meeting.
It was very nice to meet you and discuss your position as a
leasing agent.

Dawn Nusbaum
2121 Gordon Drive
Anytown

Anytown, March 24, 19XX

Mrs. Pruitt,

I am extremely grateful to you for revealing the secrets of your
profession to me during our interview this afternoon.
I will certainly contact the people whose names and addresses
you so kindly gave me, and keep you informed of my progress.
Thank you!

John Holbrook
5478 Pamona Avenue
Anytown

How do you say thank you? (continued)

Anytown, November 5, 19XX

Mr. Iles,

The interview this morning was quite pleasurable and insightful.
I anticipate making a final career decision soon, and the
information which you gave me will be very beneficial.
Much gratitude,

Norman Leonard
Rural Route 3
Anytown

Anytown, September 3, 19XX

Ms. Banks,

Your enthusiasm about the engineering field is quite contagious.
Thank you for making the time to meet with me to discuss your
career.

Bridget Harlan
7605 Pershing Road
Anytown

Anytown, January 7, 19XX

Mr. Hollings,
I enjoyed meeting with you on Wednesday, January 5, to
discuss your position as a pharmaceutical sales representative.
Although your field sounds competitive, I believe it is my career
of choice. Thank you for the names of other people whom I can
contact.

Helen Armand
786 Orchard Blvd.
Anytown

Anytown, October 12, 19XX

Mrs. Setter,
Thank you for the interview this morning.
It was a pleasure to meet you. I learned quite a few things that
I did not know about the field of agronomy.

Rich Seeley
11 Cedar Cove Circle
Anytown

What is the length of the Information phase?

The I (Information) phase usually is shorter than you might imagine.

Only four hours (a single afternoon) allows you to conduct one or two of your information interviews. This is even more remarkable because these appointments are easily set by telephone the evening before the interviews or that very morning.

If you want to explore:

- one target job, your three to five interviews should be spread out over one week at the most;

- two target jobs, your 6 to 10 interviews (three to five interviews for each job) should be spread out over two weeks at the most;

- three target jobs, your 9 to 15 interviews (three to five interviews for each job) should be spread out over three weeks at the most; or

- three target jobs and one plan B job, your 12 to 20 interviews (three to five interviews per job) should be spread out over four weeks at the most: only one month!

You will spend a maximum of one month exploring a career and job which may inspire you for the next five to seven years or maybe even all of your life!

What are the dangers of the Information phase?

The greatest danger of the PIE Method's I (Information) phase consists of accepting an information interview which turns into an employment interview (phase E).

This is tempting. This happens frequently. This practically always leads to failure!

Who assumes responsibility for the failure?

■ It is sometimes your fault.

The temptation is great when meeting a professional with whom you've obtained an information interview to explore the situation for possible employment opportunities and propel the conversation in that direction.

■ It is sometimes the fault of the interviewee.

Impressed by the quality and relevance of your questions, the interviewee sometimes forgets the true reason for your visit, and begins to discuss opportunities for employment.

■ It is sometimes the fault of both of you.

The interviewee and you, enthusiastic and passionate about the subject of the interview, both forget the goal of simply gathering information and shoot ahead to phase E (Employment).

What are the dangers of the Information phase? (continued)

This mistake, voluntary or involuntary, is a serious strategic error for four reasons.

■ Ethical

It is dishonest to be received under the pretense of obtaining information and then to take advantage of the interview to make a move toward another objective: gaining employment.

■ Effectiveness

If you request an information interview through a third party and tell yourself that you will be able to discuss employment as well, your true objective will be unclear even to yourself.

If you have not one but two objectives in mind, your interviewee may recognize this and put up his or her guard. If the interviewee perceives this ambiguity, you will quickly be made to pay for it by not getting any information at all.

■ Performance

You should be able to perform well in E (Employment) phase interviews if you have successfully completed all of your interviews in the information phase.

At the end of your information phase, you will have:

➤ relevant information on the job to which you aspire;

➤ the language of the job and field which attract you; and

➤ the arguments necessary to be convincing.

But, if during the course of the I (Information) phase, you decide to slip into the E (Employment) phase, you are committing a grave error. You are unprepared and have little chance of performing well, convincing employers, and having your target job offered to you

What are the dangers of the Information phase? (continued)

■ Deception

Sometimes, an interviewee who was deceived by someone who came under the pretense of gathering information but who in fact was looking for work sets a trap for you.

DANGER!

During the course of your interview for information with this interviewee, he or she may suggest that you slip from the I (Information) phase into the E (Employment) phase.

In this case, be firm and avoid getting trapped! Say thank you, but firmly reject this invitation. This will not reduce your chances of being offered a job later. On the contrary, this should enable you to increase your chances!

Here is some typical dialogue which you could adopt between yourself and the interviewee.

"It is interesting that you should come to see me about this kind of position because we are currently looking for a candidate to fill such a job in our organization. Would that eventually interest you?"

"Your offer is both pleasing and surprising! It is pleasing that you should consider me and I thank you. It is surprising because I am not here seeking employment but simply to gather information and verify that I can contribute positively to an organization in this position. So far, the information which I have collected is convergent and positive. I prefer, nonetheless, to continue gathering information on this position until I am 100 percent certain."

"But since you are here, why not talk to the supervisor and the director of human relations?"

"I appreciate that but we agreed on 20 minutes for this interview and we have already taken 30. I am really sorry but I have another appointment."

"What a pity!"

"Let's do it this way. As I told you, I am meeting with two or three other people in similar positions as you to discuss this field. If these meetings are positive, and I expect them to be, I will certainly contact you again."

What are the dangers of the Information phase? (continued)

■ Recommendations

To avoid possibly slipping from the I (Information) phase into the E (Employment) phase, here are some recommendations.

> ➤ Be clear with yourself. Have only one objective: to gain information, not employment.
>
> ➤ Be thorough in your questioning.
>
> ➤ Be firm in your attitude.
>
> ➤ Predetermine the length of each interview and stick to it.
>
> ➤ Go to interviews accompanied by a friend.
>
> ➤ Remember, throughout the interview, the objective which you are pursuing: gathering information
>
> ➤ Explain the PIE Method, if the situation arises. Clearly state that you wish to avoid any mistakes in these interviews which would hamper your career.
>
> ➤ Say, if it is the case, that you are experiencing a turning point in your career and this is the reason you wish to obtain information. Your interviewee will be less tempted to bring up the subject of offering you a job!

The PIE Method: E Phase (Employment phase)

What are the objectives of the Employment phase?

The main objective of the E (Employment) phase is to find a job.

This phase is centered on two objectives.

E

Objective #1 To land an interview

You could get this interview from the advertised market (responding to classified ads) or from the hidden market (making spontaneous contacts: writing letters, telephoning, cold calling …).

Objective #2 To get a job offer

During the interview, your objective is simple: to get a job offer from the interviewer. For this, you must successfully demonstrate that your competencies and talents correspond with the problems the interviewer needs solved. The I (Information) phase, which you have previously conducted, will help you convince the interviewer.

What fields do you choose?

During the course of the employment phase, you approach organizations to submit your resume or application. It is no longer a matter of going to see people to collect the information on positions which attract you or to validate the jobs which you envision.

Your objective now is to meet the organization's supervisors with whom you are going to "talk employment." These are the people from whom you wish to receive job offers.

You will encounter four possible situations.

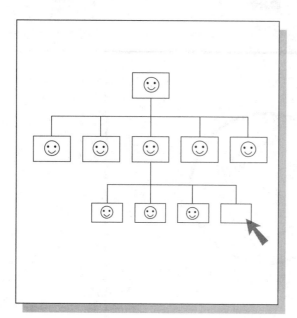

Situation #1 Very Good Luck

You contact an organization which has an open position corresponding exactly to the job you want to do.

You are indeed a lucky person. This luck is not purely coincidental though because if you would have stayed at home, this luck would not have smiled on you.

The more people you meet, the more your chances multiply for this type of good luck!

Situation #2 Very Good Luck (again!)

You contact an organization that already employs people doing the job you want to do and which is able to recruit another employee.

This happens essentially in large organizations which have a medium or long-term view.

In this case, too you have been blessed by good fortune!

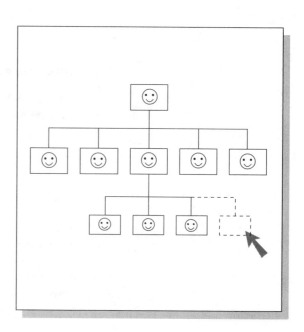

What fields do you choose? (continued)

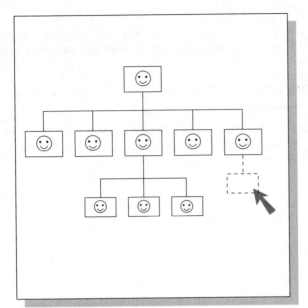

Situation #3 Very Good Luck (once again!)

You contact an organization that has no one doing the tasks of the job you envision but which creates this position.

This is an example of the rich resources of the PIE Method.

Without your visit, this creation would not have taken place. You have been the creator of it.

There is a strong chance that this post was tailor-made for you!

Situation #4 Bad Luck

You contact an organization which does not need anyone because it is already fully staffed or is not involved in the tasks that correspond to the job you envision.

Pity!

It is only a temporary setback, though.

Experience shows that this situation often produces ideas and allows you to look into other organizations or similar titles.

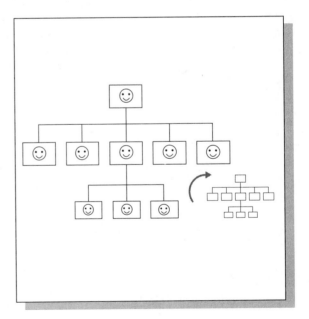

What fields do you choose? (continued)

You will approach these organizations with much more enthusiasm and confidence in yourself, if you have carried out the information phase seriously and completely.

At this stage of the PIE Method, you will feel sure of yourself. You will have acquired, thanks to the information interviews, the near certainty of perfectly fitting the position for which you are applying.

You will have the comfort of knowing in advance all of the questions which may be asked of you during the course of your interviews for employment.

Moreover, you will approach your job search enthusiastically because you will know with near certainty that the job you are looking for requires the transferable and specific skills which you are particularly fond of using.

You have all of the components of success:

➤ You know where you are going;

➤ You know 80 percent of the questions which will be asked of you; and

➤ you are enthusiastic: you possess, therefore, the secret weapon to convince others.

With whom do you arrange interviews?

The employment interviews can take place with four different people:

    A. a head hunter;

    B. the head of recruiting;

    C. the director of human resources/personnel; and

    D. the supervisor of the position to be filled.

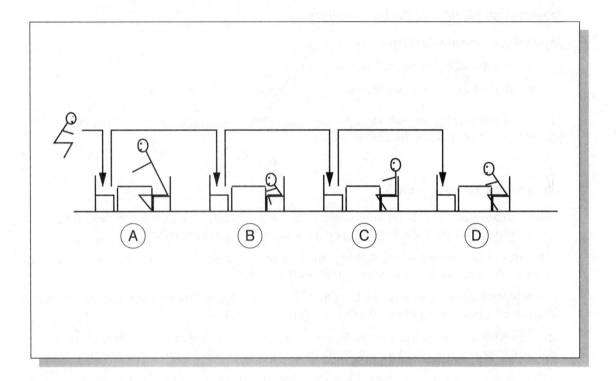

In three out of four cases—A, B, and C—you will be dealing with intermediaries.

To construct your interview strategy with these people, the three observations on the next page can be helpful to you.

With whom do you arrange interviews? (continued)

Observation #1 Distance: intermediary to supervisor

The farther removed the intermediary is from the supervisor of the job to be filled, the more this intermediary will tend to judge you on your personality traits and transferable skills rather than on your specific and technical skills.

Observation #2 Role of the intermediary

Essentially, an intermediary has a dual role:

> ➤ to get application forms filled out; and

> ➤ then to screen out candidates.

Limit your communications with this person to only information relevant to the required tasks of the open position. Don't offer anything else!

Observation #3 Be a nonrisk

When you are meeting with an intermediary, do not try to convince that person you are the best candidate. Simply show him that you are a nonrisk (a good candidate).

Demonstrate to an intermediary that you know how to execute the assignments with which you will be entrusted. To do this, give examples and achievements.

It is only when you face your future boss that you must demonstrate that you are the candidate whose profile best corresponds with the position to be filled.

Thus, the intermediary will not eliminate you. You will be included in what is referred to in technical jargon as the "short list." It contains an average of three to seven candidates.

At this stage, the boss does not eliminate anymore. His or her task is much more difficult: he or she must choose one person from the three to seven candidates selected.

With which organizations do you conduct the Employment phase?

The E (Employment) phase interviews should be conducted with all (yes, all) of the organizations in the field which interests you, which are located in your preferred geographical area, and in which you would like to work.

Consider all the organizations in the field which attracts you. Discover and verify everything you can during the course of your interviews.

There is no such thing as a bad field. There are fields which go badly and others which go rather well. Inside the fields which go badly, nearly always one or two organizations exist which have developed a niche in the market which functions admirably well. (This does not include those that only salvage the crumbs of organizations that fail!)

Which location should you choose?

The places to select for an interview for employment are diverse. They can be:

➤ nontraditional: a hotel room or suite (no, it is not a trap!);

➤ traditional: a bar, restaurant, an intermediary's office; or

➤ very traditional: conference room, lounge, office inside the organization.

It is useless to try to interpret the place selected. In general, it has more to do with common sense than strategy. If it puzzles you, don't hesitate to speak about it to your interviewer ... at the end of the interview.

Certain seasoned salespeople shrewdly use a "previsit" to be even more effective at the time of their appointment. The day before the appointment, an experienced salesperson will go look at the building in which the meeting or interview will take place. This will be done preferably at a time when the employees of the organization are going in and out of the building. This way of "testing the air" reassures the salesperson. The next day, it gives the person the feeling of arriving on familiar ground. This helps calm nerves and instill self-assurance—therefore, making the salesperson more efficient.

How do you set appointments?

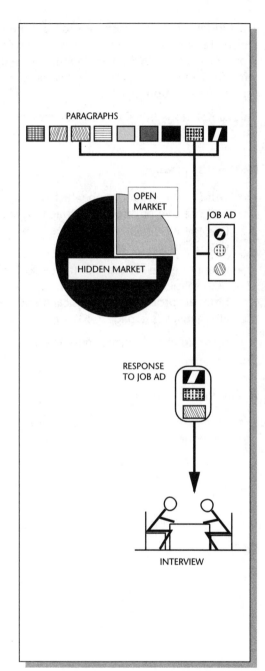

PARAGRAPHS

OPEN MARKET

HIDDEN MARKET

JOB AD

RESPONSE TO JOB AD

INTERVIEW

There are two employment markets: the open market and the hidden market. For each type of market, two corresponding ways can be used to set appointments.

The open market covers positions which are to be filled through ads placed in newspapers (about 2 or 3 positions in every 10).

The organizations which need someone publish a "job offer" ad. Anyone interested in the ad can answer it. You often find yourself confronted with intense competition.

When you answer a "job offer" ad, don't expect to be the best.

First, you must demonstrate to the organization that you are a "nonrisk." To put the odds on your side, simply underline the fact that you possess all of the characteristics which the organization requires. Read the published ad carefully and identify the criteria which define the profile of the ideal candidate—each ad averages four criteria (which we discovered by going through 1,200 ads). Then, demonstrate point by point that you have the profile required for the position, by using precise examples and figures.

You should respond to employment ads:

- in writing (either by the traditional method of a letter and resume, or by a nontraditional method: answering point by point, asking for more information, etc.);

- by telephoning the secretary or assistant of the person who will interview candidates (avoid having an interview over the telephone; only set an appointment for the interview) or;

- by presenting yourself unannounced to the organization.

How do you set appointments? (continued)

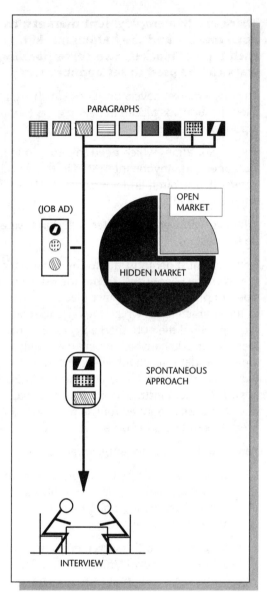

The hidden market corresponds to positions which are not advertised in the newspaper (about 7 or 8 positions in every 10). You must take the initiative yourself by making what is called a "spontaneous approach."

This can be done in a direct or indirect way.

■ **The direct way:**

- write to the organization which attracts you and cite two or three of your achievements (use paragraphs of two to three lines each for describing your achievements);

- telephone the secretary of the person you wish to meet and propose two appointment times according to the classical method of alternatives (see page 7 13); or

- show up at the organization unannounced.

■ **The indirect way:**

- go through a friend or relative who knows someone … who knows someone.

How do you set appointments? (continued)

A clever, original, and effective method consists of multiplying the interviews of the I (Information) phase to avoid conducting employment interviews as well.

Instead of conducting only three to five information interviews, do 15-20 of them. Schedule all of these interviews with the organizations in which you wish to work. Meet the people who hold the positions toward which you wish to direct yourself.

During your interviews, do not mention at any time the subject of employment. Limit yourself to only gathering information!

The following day send a thank-you card.

Then, when you have completed the tour of the organizations, write a letter to each of the people you interviewed whom you would like to meet again. Tell them that your survey was positive, thanks to the information they gave you.

Never ask for help or for strings to be pulled.

Thank them…. That is all.

The hint will be clear to your interviewees that they may recontact you if they wish or pass on the information to their supervisor or a similar organization.

An example of such a letter is given on the next page.

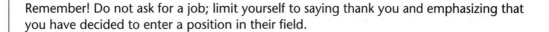

Remember! Do not ask for a job; limit yourself to saying thank you and emphasizing that you have decided to enter a position in their field.

How do you set appointments? (continued)

It is preferable to type your answer. If you have personalized stationery, use it to give your letter a more professional appearance.

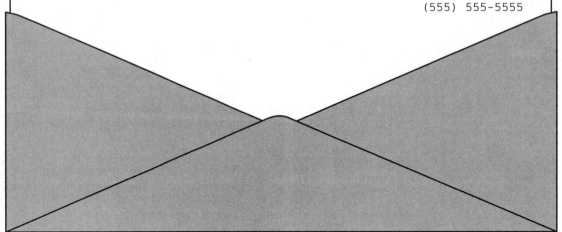

September 5, 19XX

Mr. Robert Hughes
10 Morton Avenue
Anytown, ST 00000-0000

Dear Mr. Hughes:

First of all, allow me to thank you for the interview which you granted me on July 2, 19XX.

You asked me to keep you apprised of my progress, and it is for this reason that I am writing to you. I have decided to pursue a position as a marketing assistant.

Thanks, in part, to the information and the names of contacts which you gave me, I have completed my survey. It was very positive.

I have verified that I would be able to genuinely contribute positively to an organization as a marketing assistant. I am now prepared to embark on my campaign for employment.

Thank you once again for the help and kindness which you offered me.

Yours faithfully,

Deborah Jones
7 Banks Avenue
Anytown, ST 00000-0000
(555) 555-5555

How long do these interviews last?

The length of employment interviews is determined most often by the person who receives you. The length varies depending on whether you are in the open market or the hidden market.

■ The Open Market

If you have answered an ad, you will find yourself on the open market. In this case, the length of interview is nearly always determined by the recruiting organization. When an organization places an ad, it usually interviews between five and fifteen candidates.

Two types of interviews are commonly practiced: the individual interview and the group interview.

Tactic #1 The individual interview

If you are received individually, the first interview will last between 20 minutes (if it is very short) and one hour (if it is very long).

Tactic #2 The group interview

If you are received in a group with several candidates or several recruiters, the first interview will generally last from 1 1/2 to 3 hours.

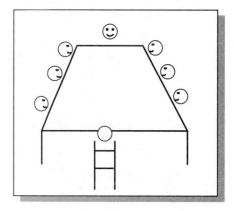

How long do these interviews last? (continued)

■ The Hidden Market

If you approach organizations on the hidden market, the length of these interviews varies. They are usually short because these interviews are often individual ones. The interview length can be set by telephone with the assistant or secretary of the person you wish to meet.

Therefore, you have the choice between two strategies regarding the length of these interviews:

> ➤ the successive interviews strategy, and

> ➤ the elastic interview strategy.

Strategy #1 The successive interviews

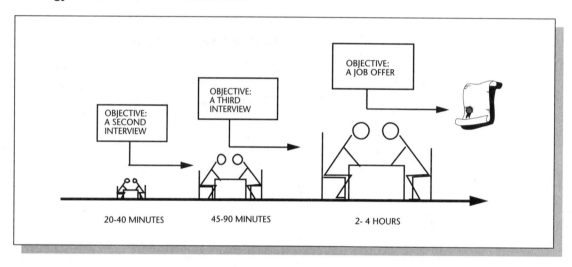

In this case, each interview is a pretext for the next interview.

The first interview is generally short. Use it to:

> ➤ emphasize, through precise examples and figures, contributions that you can offer to the organization with which you are interviewing; and

> ➤ ask relevant questions which are going to give your interviewer the desire to see you a second time, then a third time … until a job offer is made.

This method is advantageous because it allows you to:

> ➤ use a sensible approach; and

> ➤ prepare for following interviews (thanks to the information collected during previous interviews).

If you decide to utilize the successive interview strategy, write down ideas for solving problems, general remarks, and propositions between each interview. Present them during the next interview. This will demonstrate to your interviewer that:

> ➤ you are interested in the organization's problems;

> ➤ you are already getting involved in management; and

> ➤ you will not be an "extra burden" but an "extra hand" which will help lighten his or her workload.

How long do these interviews last? (continued)

Strategy #2 The elastic interview

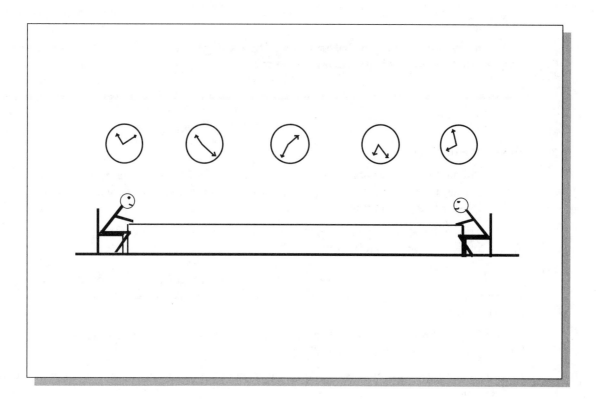

This strategy consists of agreeing on a first interview and purposely avoiding setting a time limit.

During this interview, be certain to pique your interviewer's interest sufficiently so that he or she will want to spend more time getting to know you.

The interview, therefore, lasts for two, three, maybe even four hours. The major advantage of this strategy is the flexibility it allows you. It provides you with enough time to review all of the areas in which your interviewer has needs and in which you can intervene to help.

How many interviews should you have?

A correlation exists between the number of interviews you have with the same organization and an increasing chance of getting a job offer for the position being discussed.

> **The more the number of interviews with an organization increases, the more your chances of a job proposal increase.**

This is for two reasons:

➤ The fact that an organization wishes to see you again is in itself a good sign. You can be certain that you interest them. Successive interviews will result in validating or invalidating certain traits in your personality;

➤ The multiplication of interviews creates a connection and confidence which work positively toward a job offer.

Nevertheless, multiplication of interviews must not signify increasing the length of each interview. Avoid, if the interviews multiply, giving the impression of settling in with the people receiving you.

If you feel that these interviews are multiplying because you are an excellent source of information (and are being "pumped"), be careful.

Do not hesitate to keep your distance and not reveal all your specific skills.

What questions should you ask?

Interview strategy

Thanks to the I (Information) phase interviews, you have "plowed" the ground and already know practically 85 percent of the subjects and questions which you may be asked about during an interview for employment. In phase E (Employment), you will reap the fruits of your past efforts.

Phase E (Employment) of the PIE Method consists simply of applying your efforts through the "needs-benefits" approach.

This extremely simple method is played in three moves.

Move #1 Your questions

Ask your interviewer relevant questions so that the needs in his or her department or organization are revealed to you.

Avoid using the word "problem." Organizations never have problems; rather they have challenges to rise to, opportunities to seize, aspects to restructure, priorities to concentrate on, etc.

Move #2 The interviewer's needs

Intrigued by your questions, the interviewer cites the needs in the area which you wish to join.

Encourage the interviewer. Start the ball rolling by stating examples of needs which you collected during your information interviews. This will help him or her overcome any hesitancy.

Move #3 Your solutions

Once the needs are exposed, show the interviewer, with the help of examples drawn from your past, that you can benefit the organization.

For each need cited, demonstrate an achievement you accomplished which proves your competency to find the solution.

What questions should you ask? (continued)

➤ First of all, emphasize your seriousness. Make your interviewer see that you are a "nonrisk." Especially highlight your ability to solve problems. Do not emphasize your preference for taking the initiative too much.

➤ Then, change your tone. Show that you like to take the initiative and that each time you do, you take care to do it with the greatest security.

It is only when no more than two or three candidates are in the running that you must do everything in your power to show that you are the best!

A final word of advice! Remember at all times that organizations never hire strangers. At best, they hire semistrangers. If a recruiter has the choice between two candidates, he or she will always choose the person who is less of a stranger, even if that person is not the best.

Thus, if you apply for a position which is relatively unfamiliar to you, pay particular attention to the vocabulary, jargon, and figures used. You do not want to appear as a stranger to the field.

The I (Information) phase of the PIE Method will have sufficiently prepared you for confronting the people doing the job which appeals to you. You will know, therefore, the language and jargon of the profession. The applications and methods used most often in this job will not be a secret to you. Make good use of them!

Should you take notes?

Everything said about taking notes in the I (Information) phase applies to the E (Employment) phase.

If promises made to you during an interview seem too good to be true, have them confirmed in writing.

Two formulas are possible. You could:

1. propose that you or the interviewer summarize the terms of the interview in writing; or

2. ask the interviewer to include them in a written proposal or in the contract he or she plans to offer you.

If you are embarrassed to bring up this subject, use the classic formula which consists of saying:

"Just for the record, how would you like to handle this? Would you like me to summarize in writing the terms of our interview, or would you prefer to do it yourself?"

If the interviewer asks you to simply believe what is said, or worse, if he or she questions your lack of faith, do not back down. Say, for example:

"As a professional habit, I always put down the important things in writing."

or better:

"I have every confidence in you, but you may be promoted and your successor—who will become my boss—will have promised me nothing and I will have no documentation to which to refer."

How do you obtain names?

Whom should you approach?

Ideally, approach those people in an organization who can best appreciate what you have to offer. This is not easy!

To obtain names, two effective methods are frequently used.

Method #1 The telephone

Call the organization which interests you. Once on line with the switchboard, ask for the person's name with such and such responsibility.

If you cannot uncover the information you are looking for, use your imagination. Here are two examples from hundreds which have been reported to us.

First example: **"The pretext of an invitation"**

"I am sending an invitation to the person in charge of employee travel in your organization. Could you please give me the exact spelling of this person's name and his or her precise title?"

Second example: **"Speak the lie to know the truth"**

"I need to send something to the person in your organization who is in charge of travel—a Mrs. Phillips I believe—could you please tell me if her name is spelled with one 'l' or two?"

Method #2 A friend or relative

Use a friend or relative who works in the field which interests you.

Verify the name you have been given and the correct spelling.

How do you build a network?

Three avenues allow you to get interviews:

- ➤ answering ads;
- ➤ direct approach; and
- ➤ the "false/true answer" approach.

■ **Answering ads**

Job ads can be found in newspapers and magazines sold in stores and newsstands or which you receive.

We have the tendency to limit ourselves to a restricted number of publications. We unconsciously apply the 20/80 rule and consult only the 20 percent of publications in which 80 percent of the ads are published.

Some job offers (the remaining 20 percent) for interesting positions are published in rarely consulted reviews (80 percent of publications). Therefore, very few candidates answer these ads. The organizations who advertise them, which are then confronted with a very limited number of candidates, often ask all the candidates to interview. Therefore, your chances of getting an interview for these positions are much higher.

Do not neglect these publications.

■ **Direct approach**

In the hidden market, drop the belief that your resume will interest nearly all of the organizations in the field which attracts you. These organizations may not have a vacant position, but dynamic organizations are always interested in candidates who have something to offer them. They are constantly on the lookout for new ideas.

Do not hesitate to approach them.

How do you build a network? (continued)

open market

hidden market

■ **The "false/true answer" approach**

This technique is very clever. Here is how it works. Suppose that organization XYZ places a job ad for position A in field B. If organization XYZ in this field needs to create or fill position A, then other organizations in the same field are probably confronted with the same problem. So, using a professional directory or telephone book, identify organizations in the same field, approach them and offer your services for position A.

Here are two examples illustrating this approach.

Example #1 "Regional manager"

In a national daily newspaper, an organization placed an ad for a regional manager. This organization is medium-sized and is in the mechanical engineering field.

Systematically approach all the organizations in this field operating in the geographical area which you prefer. Offer your services to them as a regional manager.

Example #2

An organization places an ad for a sales representative. The organization is a small company specializing in health food.

Approach all the smaller-sized organizations in the health food industry. Offer these organizations your services as a sales representative.

How do you build a network? (continued)

■ **What do you do if you are rejected after being interviewed?**

If an organization with which you have had one or more interviews rejects your application, recontact them.

Do not in any way ask why they did not hire you, but proceed in five steps.

First step

Acknowledge the fact that they have found a candidate whose profile perfectly matches the position. Congratulate them on this accomplishment.

Make it clear that you especially appreciated the quality of your relationship during the interview process and the care with which they handled your application.

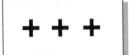

Second step

Ask them to name two or three strong points they noted about you during the interview process.

Third step

Next, ask them to say if they think that the position which interests you matches these strong points.

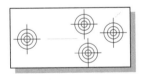

Fourth step

Then ask them if they know what would be, if the case arose, some different positions you could approach.

Fifth step

Finally, ask them for an opinion on your resume and other documents you used as well as on your behavior during the interview process.

How do you say thank you?

During phase E (Employment) and contrary to phases P (Pleasure) and I (Information), reflect before saying thank you. Your thanks are neither necessary nor automatic but well-thought-out and strategic.

You have two choices.

■ Choice #1 Don't write

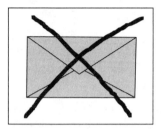

Don't write to say nothing. A letter which tries to say, "I would be delighted to work for you, and I deeply hope that you will retain my application … ," must be well worded to be effective.

On one hand, you must show your determination and motivation. On the other hand, you should avoid giving the impression that you are hanging on desperately to this organization as if it was your only hope.

■ Choice #2 Write

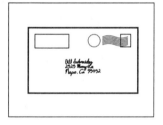

You could send a letter in which you precisely state the reasons which attracted you to the position, if they are genuine and supported by examples. You can conclude your letter by stating one or two achievements which show that you are the right person for the position. The most important aspect of the letter is that it rings true. Make sure that its tone is neither flattering nor begging. An example of such a letter is given to you on the next page.

How do you say thank you? (continued)

Send a thank-you letter after the interview.

November 24, 19XX

Miss Emily Thacker
6787 Higgins Lane
Anytown, ST 00000-0000

Dear Miss Thacker,

I am writing to you following the interview you granted me on
November 16, 19XX at 3:00 p.m.

Allow me to say that I particularly appreciated the spirit in which
our discussion took place.

THEN SAY ...

———— EITHER ————

Three aspects of the position particularly captured my attention:

The financial …
Project figures for …
Yearly …

———— OR ————

Two elements in particular attracts me to this position in your
organization:

The importance of post-sale service …
The flexible scheduling…

As agreed, we will contact one another after December 5, 19XX.

Yours faithfully,

Michelle Thompson
875 West Street
Anytown, ST 00000-0000
(555) 555-5555

What is the length of the Employment phase?

Determine three possible lengths for your E (Employment) phase. This is the phase of the PIE Method devoted exclusively to finding a job.

➤ **"Flash" duration:** The flash duration is certainly what everyone wishes for during the job search. These very short or lightening job search campaigns last between two and six weeks.

➤ **"Ideal" duration:** The ideal duration corresponds to the time limit you are willing to cope with before your job search becomes a nerve-grinding obsession or trauma.

➤ **"Long" duration:** A long duration is determined by your financial resources. It is the longest period for which you are capable of supporting yourself without falling into financial catastrophe.

 Be careful!

A long duration can become a major handicap in your job search campaign. If you think that your search runs the risk of becoming too long, be careful and protect yourself.

You can take two precautions.

Precaution #1 Volunteer

Volunteer your time for a philanthropic activity, so as to be able to:

➤ continue to function intellectually, not to rust, and also to keep your internal clock intact; and

➤ demonstrate to a prospective employer, who might question the length of your search, that you have remained active during this period, and therefore, operational.

Do these philanthropic or charitable activities by offering your talents and time to:

➤ a club which you frequent;

➤ a nonprofit association; or

➤ a project with social value.

Precaution #2 Envision a plan B job

Regardless of the duration you envision, always have a plan B job in mind. Know what type of job you can fall back on if you don't get an offer for the job which appeals to you most.

You must not invent this plan B job at the last minute; you should foresee it during the information phase.

Remember! Experience shows that the average job search lasts twice as long as one expects.

What are the dangers of the Employment phase?

■ Negotiate on several fronts

The major danger that you encounter during the employment phase is being viewed as a job seeker.

Do everything within your power so that your interviewer sees you more as a "provider of services."

Do not limit yourself to negotiating with only one organization (diagram #1). Conduct negotiations with several organizations. Briefly mention to each interviewer that you are pursuing various paths. Make each one aware that his or her organization is not the only one that you have contacted and with which you are negotiating.

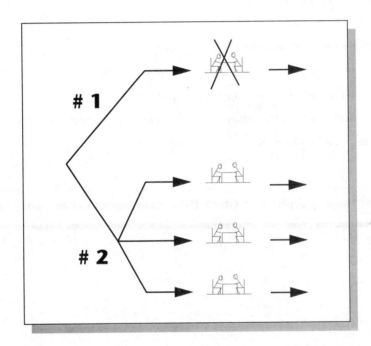

Respect two essential negotiation principles:

➤ mention the number of possible competitors with which you are in contact but do not overdo it. Cite these quickly and subtlely;

➤ reassure the interviewer with whom you are meeting. Tell the interviewer, if it is the case, that you prefer his or her organization. If it is not the case, mention the two or three aspects of the organization that you appreciate.

What are the dangers of the Employment phase? (continued)

■ Take advantage of each interview

Always keep a positive view of the interviews that await you.

Be wary of negative views which are incited by the belief that only two possible outcomes exist.

1. The good: to get a firm job offer

2. The bad: to leave empty-handed

A positive outlook will ensure that you win no matter what happens. Persuade yourself that any interview can bring you, among other things, the possibility to:

➤ keep your morale intact;

➤ gather information;

➤ receive an offer for part-time employment;

➤ get your name in the organization's employment files;

➤ negotiate a contract for temporary employment;

➤ get an indication of the salary which you can expect in the position; and

➤ be offered a full-time job.

> **Be one of those people who think that all experiences are enriching.**

8

SOME GOLDEN RULES AND ADVICE TO ENSURE YOUR SUCCESS

Voila! You know practically everything necessary to succeed. Before launching yourself into the job market, take a final glance at the golden rules and the ways to resolve situations which you will encounter during your search.

Some Golden Rules and Advice to Ensure Your Success

The Golden Rules of Success

Thousands of people have practiced the PIE Method for their job search.

From the experiences of hundreds of job seekers, we have selected the best advice ... 12 golden rules.

These rules are presented to you on the following pages. They can make your job search easier. They will help you avoid falling into the classic traps that any method produces.

The PIE Method has proven itself. It has successfully passed the test of time. Take advantage of it!

Do the PIE

It is not necessary to bring someone along for PIE Method interviews, but it tends to make things more agreeable!

It is preferable to conduct your surveys with a friend (except in phase E). Choose someone whom you respect and with whom you enjoy spending time!

To convince the other person, explain the PIE Method and let him or her decide from that.

Listed below are the advantages of going with someone and the disadvantages of going alone.

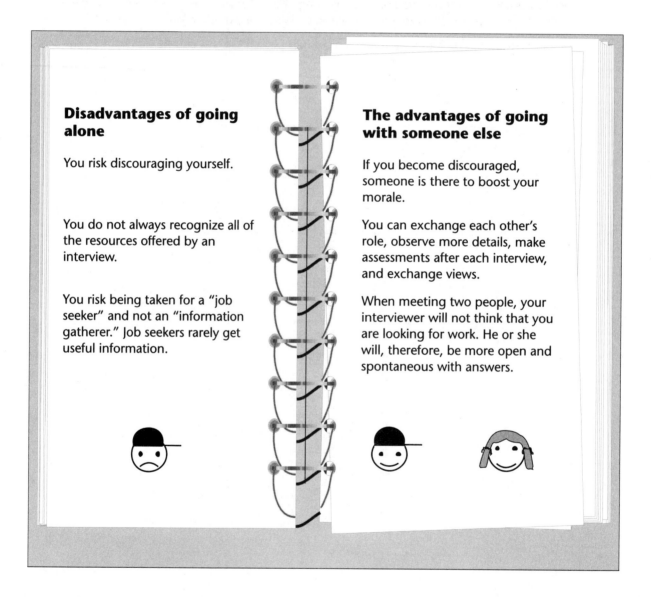

Disadvantages of going alone

You risk discouraging yourself.

You do not always recognize all of the resources offered by an interview.

You risk being taken for a "job seeker" and not an "information gatherer." Job seekers rarely get useful information.

The advantages of going with someone else

If you become discouraged, someone is there to boost your morale.

You can exchange each other's role, observe more details, make assessments after each interview, and exchange views.

When meeting two people, your interviewer will not think that you are looking for work. He or she will, therefore, be more open and spontaneous with answers.

Stick to the rules

There are not many questions in the PIE Method. Adopt the sequence which was presented to you.

They have been conceived to allow you to flow from one phase to the other: from P to I or from I to E.

You are free to modify the questions by removing certain ones, including others, or rethinking the order. Do it only if it helps you achieve, without risk, your objective more easily and rapidly.

Behind the questions of each phase is the secret of their effectiveness. It is a forward progression known as "in the drawer." This trick is readily visible in the "PIE . . CTOGRAM" presented below.

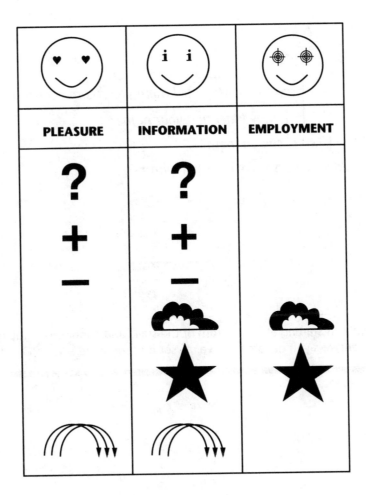

Proceed progressively to obtain names

Take certain precautions when you begin your search for names to build your PIE network.

➤ Ask for names of people who work in the same field (in phase P) or who hold the same position (in phase I) as your interviewer. Avoid being given names of organizations. You want people's names!

➤ Proceed in stages. Utilize the "stairs" or "escalation" method which is frequently used for negotiating. The interviewer will be impressed by your tactfulness and discretion.

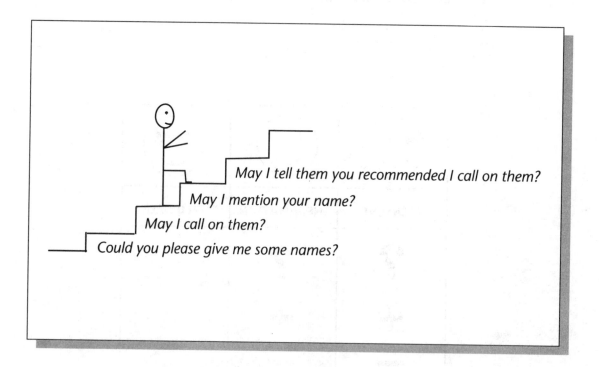

May I tell them you recommended I call on them?

May I mention your name?

May I call on them?

Could you please give me some names?

Ask the questions starting at the bottom of the stairs and continue climbing the steps as long as the answers you get are positive. As soon as someone says "NO," stop climbing!

Go in person; do not use the telephone

In dire circumstances, use the telephone to conduct an interview. But for most situations, do not carry out your PIE interviews by telephone.

Experience shows that during a face-to-face interview:

➤ the positive and negative aspects of a job are more detailed and exposed than during a telephone interview;

➤ information on the atmosphere of the position and the organization is much more significant;

➤ the theoretical and practical sides of the position make more sense;

➤ the recommendations for researching the position, obtaining names, and constructing a specific strategy are much more precise, useful, and effective;

➤ and, above all, names are practically never given over the telephone.

Speak the language of your interviewer

■ Principles

According to Richard Bolles, who is a well-respected expert on job search techniques, organizations do not hire strangers.

To a recruiter or interviewer, a stranger is someone who does not belong to their field or profession.

However, do not be discouraged if you are not part of the field that you wish to integrate.

If you have not worked or been educated in the field which attracts you, do not despair.

You can at least become a "semistranger" by mitigating your differences. To do this, study the practices and standards of the field which you wish to integrate. Learn to speak their language and jargon.

Interviewers will often be surprised by the incongruity of your knowledge of the vocabulary of their field and your apparent lack of experience in it. Tell them that you have done your homework. Simply explain that the reason you are so familiar with their position and field is because you have acquired the knowledge from books and through discussions with others in the field.

Speak the language of your interviewer (continued)

■ Vocabulary

In the course of your I (Information) phase interviews, you must discover, understand, and memorize the language of the position and field which attracts you. During your E (Employment) phase interviews, you must use it.

Here are some examples which show how language differs from one field to another. We have selected three fields in which different vocabulary is used to refer to:

➤ services/products;

➤ clients; and

➤ suppliers.

	BANK	HOTEL	PHARMACEUTICAL COMPANY
Services/products referred to as …	• Credit • Loans • Financing • Accounts	• Accommodations • Conferences • Banquets • Catering	• Medicine • Remedies • Vaccines • Drugs
Clients are called …	• Institutions • Societies • Accounts • Individual Customers	• Groups • Patrons • Guests • Businesses	• Wholesalers • Patients • Consumers • Dealers
Suppliers are identified as …	• Institutions • Banks • Markets • Depositors	• Dealers • Distributors • Salespeople • Contracts	• Manufacturers • Producers • Slaughterhouses (for example, insulin is extracted from animals), • Agricultural Suppliers (for example, many plant extracts are used in medicine)

Advice for mastering the language of the field which attracts you:

➤ discover the typical vocabulary used in the position and field which attract you during your information interviews;

➤ practice using this vocabulary during information interviews. This will help you obtain more "insider" information. When an interviewer hears you speaking the language of the field, he or she gains confidence in you … and you gain confidence in yourself; and

➤ use all of the vocabulary you have learned during employment interviews to get job offers in less time.

Speak the language of your interviewer (continued)

■ Key figures

Each job and field has key figures and numbers. The I (Information) phase of the PIE Method will help you discover them.

For example:

> ➤ a doctor treats 15-30 patients per day;
>
> ➤ a highly specialized consultant advises 60-120 days a year;
>
> ➤ an industrial product salesperson carries out 1-4 client visits per day;
>
> ➤ a salesperson of products which are consumed widely calls on 15-30 businesses per day;
>
> ➤ a secretary types 4-6 letters per hour;
>
> ➤ a draftsman executes 10 plans per week;
>
> ➤ a computer scientist sets up an invoicing system in one month;
>
> ➤ a switchboard receptionist can answer 90 calls an hour;
>
> ➤ a teacher has 15-30 hours of courses each week; and
>
> ➤ a retail salesperson sells 10-25 pieces of clothing in one day.

Awareness of these figures during employment interviews, will show your interviewer that:

> ➤ you do not ignore any aspect of a job;
>
> ➤ your are probably ready to handle this position; and
>
> ➤ you possess a good capacity to adapt.

Get names

During the P (Pleasure) and I (Information) phases, ask your interviewee if he or she will give you names. Be sure that you obtain the names of people and not the names of organizations.

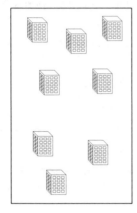

If the interviewee gives you a list of names of organizations, say thank you.

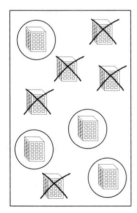

Then ask that person to point out three to five preferred organizations on the list.

Finally, for each of the organizations indicated, ask for the name of someone who works there.

Overcome resistance

Here are some proven ideas and advice which will help you successfully overcome any resistance you encounter in the **P (Pleasure)** or **I (Information)** phases.

➤ Have a third party arrange your visit by telephone and recommend you.

➤ Propose two choices of appointment times (cite second, the one which you prefer or which has the most chance of being accepted).

➤ Offer to meet for the appointment about 10 minutes before the person normally takes lunch or leaves the office (11:50 or 4:50).

➤ Indicate a specific time. Don't say "around 10 to 20 minutes," say "15 minutes."

➤ Make sure that your face and body exude confidence and calmness.

➤ On arrival, smile and stay quiet for a moment. Your calm demeanor will communicate positively.

➤ Never invade boundaries. To overcome them, ask questions which the person setting the boundaries wants to answer. (For example, ask the person what he or she likes most about the job!)

➤ Identify yourself. Say your name at least twice. Spell it.

➤ Explain the PIE Method briefly and clearly as well as the goal of the interview.

➤ State, in advance if necessary, the questions you wish to ask.

➤ Go on someone's recommendation. (It's very easy when you approach your 2nd, 3rd, 4th... interview).

➤ Go to the interviews empty-handed.

➤ Pronounce your interviewee's name correctly.

➤ Mention the names of people whom you have already met, especially if they are well-known and respected.

Feel obligated not to let go

The PIE Method is a kind of version of the art of getting caught in your own trap.

Your first step will be the most difficult. This will be the first interview obtained and conducted.

Afterwards, you will feel bound or morally obliged to meet the people whose names have been kindly given to you!

Encourage confidence

To encourage the people you meet to have confidence in you, have confidence in them.

Mistrust is conveyed first (but fortunately rarely) by the refusal to receive you.

If you are admitted by a person on his or her guard, you will receive only general and banal information.

Here are a few recommendations that will help you instill confidence in your interviewer.

➤ Identify yourself by name when you arrive, and spell it.

➤ Keep smiling (but your smile must not look stupid or fake).

➤ State the goal of the interview or clearly explain the PIE Method. The more you tell the truth, the more confidence will be established.

➤ Do not take notes.

➤ Remain calm. Have reassuring gestures, a firm delivery, and a quiet and determined attitude.

Watch your language

An inadequate vocabulary closes doors and makes your interviewer distrustful.

SO ...
DON'T SAY ...

I am doing a survey ...

I would like to pass some time with ...

I would like it if we could discuss ...

I need a brief moment ...

This will last from 10 to 20 minutes ...

In the morning ... whenever you like ...

I am looking for a job ...

I am in the stage of looking for a career ...

I am unemployed ...

I am out of work ...

I am looking for my first job ...

I would like to check ...

RATHER SAY ...

I am doing a personal project on ...

I would like to ask you six questions ...

I want to know four things ...

We need 10 minutes ...

A quarter of an hour will be enough ...

At 11:50 for 10 minutes ... at 5:50 for 10 minutes ...

I am faced with a major choice ...

In the context of career management training ...

I am contemplating two different occupations ...

I am at a crossroads ...

I am facing an important decision ...

I am attempting to validate ...

Be determined

If you doubt yourself ... others will distrust you.

However, during the course of your PIE Method interviews, avoid appearing too sure of yourself. Do not give the impression of someone who is overly confident or conceited—"bigheaded"—but give the impression of being very determined.

You will convey this about yourself if your ideas are clear and you have one to three well-defined objectives in mind.

Your determination is often revealed by what you say.

For example:

DO NOT SAY ...

I do not know if my job actually pleases me ...

I am thinking of changing jobs ...

I am not sure that the job you do would please me, and that is why ...

I would really like to become a consultant ...

RATHER SAY ...

I have decided to choose a new path ...

In order to precisely determine how I can contribute to an organization in this field ...

I would like to ask you six questions ...

I will soon be at a crossroads ...

Very soon, I will be confronted with a choice of three possibilities, and your opinion would be helpful to me ...

In two or three years, I am going to make a career change ...

I have decided to become ...

I want to verify my decision to ...

Do not pose a threat

You may fear that the people you approach in the information phase will perceive you as a threat or as a possible source of a leak.

To calm anxieties or fears, tell them, if needed, that the decision or professional change you envision will not take place in the near future but sometime down the road.

For example, say:

> ➤ Sometime in the future, I envision directing myself toward a job similar to yours …

> ➤ It is possible that sometime during my career, I will decide to choose a position similar to the one you hold …

> ➤ One of the two professional goals I count on realizing is to hold a position like yours …

Problems and Solutions

■ Appointments Deferred

Problem: The people whom you call for interviews are unavailable this week. Appointments are offered to you for a later date.

Solution: Accept them. Consider that this stage consists of two parts: the theoretical part and the practical part. The practical part can last more than 12 weeks after the theoretical part has concluded.

■ Barrier Created

Problem: An assistant or receptionist creates a barrier.

Solution: Before going to the organization which interests you, call and ask the switchboard for the name and office location of the person you wish to interview. When you arrive at the reception area, give the name and office of this person. Another avenue is to ask the person creating the barrier the questions you want your interviewee to answer. If the person is embarrassed by his or her inability to answer, the barrier may miraculously disappear.

■ Contacts Located Too Far Away

Problem: The people whose names are given to you as contacts are located too far away for you to contact.

Solution: Use the rebound or boomerang technique. Write or call these people and ask them if they have friends or relatives in the field which attracts you who live in or near your geographical area.

■ Insufficient Number of Names Given

Problem: Interviewee provides you with no names for future contacts or only one.

Solution: After asking for two or three names and receiving none or only one, renew your request. Establish and maintain eye contact and keep, in a conspicous manner, a pen in hand ready to write!

■ Interviewee Fears a Long Interview

Problem: Your interviewee does not think you will keep to the stated time limit. He or she is reluctant because you said: "I would like to discuss... for a while with you."

Solution: Do not say, "I would like to see you for a while around 3:30." Rather, be more precise, "I would like to meet with you for 10 minutes. How's 5:50 for you?"

Problems and Solutions (continued)

■ Interviewee Fears Content of Your Questions

Problem: Your interviewee hesitates to meet with you after you say, "I have a few questions to ask you."

Solution: Always be precise, "I have four questions to ask you" (phase P) or "I have six questions to ask you" (phase I). If the person is still reluctant, state your questions.

■ Interviewee Absent

Problem: The receptionist or office manager tells that you the person you wish to interview is absent.

Solution: Prior to your appointment or direct contact, call to verify that the person you wish to interview is there before showing up unannounced at his or her organization. But remember to avoid conducting interviews by telephone.

■ Interviewee Busy

Problem: Your interviewee is too busy to meet with you.

Solution: Suggest meeting for only 10 minutes. But for those 10 minutes to be profitable, suggest that they take place immediately before lunchtime or quitting time at the end of the day. For example, say: "Can we meet for 10 minutes at 11:50 a.m.?" If the interviewee says, "I am very busy," this may signify that he or she is hesitant about the length of the interview or the content of your questions. You can alleviate such fears by stating each question you plan to ask.

■ Interviewee Pressed for Time

Problem: At the beginning of the interview your interviewee seems hurried.

Solution: If in the first minutes of the interview you sense that your interviewee is pressed for time, suggest shortening the predetermined length of the interview or postponing it to a later date.

■ Interviewee Too Talkative

Problem: Your interviewee spends too much time on one or all of the questions you ask.

Solution: Remind your interviewee about the stipulated length of the interview and explain that you still have other questions to ask. If you feel that the time spent answering one question is too long, gently interrupt your interviewee by explaining that time is limited and you would still like to ask a few more questions.

Problems and solutions (continued)

■ Interviewee Misunderstands Your Objective

Problem: Your interviewer hesitates, asks questions, and basically doesn't understand your objective.

Solution: Explain the principles of the PIE Method, the phase which you are in (P or I), and the questions you wish to ask. Stress the fact that you are at a career crossroads and your objective is to validate a target by verifying that you can contribute positively to an organization in your chosen field.

■ List of Organizations Offered

Problem: The person interviewed gives you a list of organizations to contact instead of people's names.

Solution: Do not ask your interviewee if he or she knows other organizations in the field which interests you. Instead, ask for the names of two or three people you can contact for more information. Repeat the word "people" two or three times, if necessary. If the person still gives you a list of organizations, thank him or her. Then say that lack of time prevents you from approaching all of these organizations. Ask the interviewee to point out the three or five organizations considered to be the most representative. Finally, ask for the names of people to contact in each of them.

■ Names Not Given

Problem: Your interviewee does not give you names of people to contact to continue your PIE survey.

Solution: The tendency of your interviewee to give you names frequently correlates directly to amount of attention you have paid during the interview. Always appear interested in what your interviewee is saying. Give him or her your undivided attention.

This may occur with distrusting people, unsure of themselves. If the interviewee is self-employed or in charge of a small business, ask him or her to whom they refer clients when they are overloaded or on holiday leave. If the interviewee is a salaried employee, ask which colleague he or she would want to be seated next to during a conference covering their field. Before asking for names, say to your interviewee that you realize he or she knows the field very well … and therefore, knows many fellow professionals.

■ Other Interviewee Offered

Problem: The person whom you want to interview directs you to another person in the organization.

Solution: Clearly explain that you wish to meet with him or her personally to learn how he or she perceives the position and field which attracts you.

Problems and Solutions (continued)

■ Poor Information Provided

Problem: The information you receive is brief and banal.

Solution: This often occurs with the first or second person interviewed. To get better answers during subsequent interviews, start the ball rolling by making the interviewee privy to what the others told you (without, of course, betraying secrets). This will build confidence in your motives and encourage openness. The more people you meet, the more complete the information will be.

■ Refusal to Be Received

Problem: The person you contact by telephone is friendly but unavailable or refuses to see you.

Solution: Insist on being received and propose two dates (alternative technique), one this week and one the following week. Although it is not advisable, you can, if the situation demands it, practice the PIE Method by telephone. But the knowledge you gain from telephone interviews will be less complete. A face-to-face meeting usually allows you to easily get names of people in the field which attracts you. This is not the case during most telephone conversations.

■ Resume Requested

Problem: The person whom you contact asks you to send a resume.

Solution: Avoid approaching the organization as a job seeker—go only as an information seeker. Respond to the request for a resume by saying something like: "I have not started my job search yet; I am actually at a crossroads. I see three different paths to pursuing the next step in my career, and I would like to meet you in order to choose the right one."

■ Telephone Interview Offered

Problem: Your interviewee prefers to give you information over the phone instead of in a face-to-face meeting.

Solution: Even a short face-to-face meeting is preferable to a telephone interview. Never start asking questions over the telephone when using the PIE Method. Propose to either reduce the interview length by 10 or 15 minutes or to reschedule it for another date.

■ You Are Late for an Interview

Problem: You arrive late for an appointment because another one lasted longer than expected.

Solution: Allow extra time between interviews. Because your interviewee may be quite enthusiastic when answering your questions, the time taken to answer them often extends beyond the predetermined length of the interview.

Problems and Solutions (continued)

■ "We're Not Hiring"

Problem: The interviewer tells you the organization is not hiring.

Solution: Clearly explain that you are not seeking employment. Avoid phrases like: "I will soon be finishing my master's degree," or "I will soon be leaving my company."

■ You Become Discouraged

Problem: You discourage yourself.

Solution: Find one or two partners to conduct the PIE Method with you. This will help you maintain your morale and allows you to exchange impressions and ideas after the interviews. If your morale is really low one afternoon because it is already 1:00 p.m. and you have not set up any interviews, drop it. Do something else. Avoid going to meet someone who might be able to help you if your spirits are low.